The Frontline

Ché Walker studied acting at Webber Douglas. His first play, *Been So Long*, premiered at the Royal Court Theatre in 1998 before being translated and produced worldwide. His second play, *Flesh Wound*, premiered in 2003 at the Royal Court, winning both the George Devine Award and an Arts Council Young Writer Award. Other plays include *Crazy Love* for Paines Plough/Oran Mor (2007) and his translation of Akos Nemeth's *Car Thieves* for National Theatre/Birmingham Rep (2004). Directing work includes *Balm in Gilead*, *Hot L Baltimore*, *Mouthful of Birds* (RADA), *Achidi J's Final Hours*, *Etta Jenks* (Finborough Theatre), and *The Rootz Spectacular* (Belgrade Theatre, Coventry). Ché was born and raised in North West London, where he still lives and works.

CHÉ WALKER

The Frontline

ff

faber and faber

First published in 2008
by Faber and Faber Limited
Bloomsbury House,
74–77 Great Russell Street, London WC1B 3DA

Typeset by Country Setting, Kingsdown, Kent CT14 8ES
Printed and bound by CPI Group (UK) Ltd, Croydon, CR0 4YY

A CIP record for this book
is available from the British Library

ISBN 978-0-571-24472-0

for my mother

ANN MITCHELL

The Frontline was first performed at Shakespeare's Globe, Bankside, London, on 6 July 2008. The cast, in order of appearance, was as follows:

Beth Golda Rosheuvel
Violet Jo Martin
Erkenwald John Stahl
Ragdale Paul Copley
Mahmoud Kevork Malikyan
Donna Sally Bretton
Marcus Mo Sesay
Miruts Beru Tessema
Mordechai Thurrock Trystan Gravelle
Benny Danny Lee Wynter
Jimmy Matthew Newtion
Salim Kurt Egyiawan
Seamus Paul Lloyd
Kurt Peter Hamilton Dyer
Polish Jodie Jodie McNee
Casey Kellie Bright
Elliot Ashley Rolfe
Cockburn Robert Gwilym
Carlton Huss Garbiya
Val Lorraine Stanley
Jayson Ben Bishop
Roderique Fraser James
Babydoll Naana Agyei-Ampadu

Directed by Matthew Dunster
Designed by Paul Wills
Composed by Olly Fox
Songs by Arthur Darvill, Olly Fox and Ché Walker
Choreographed by Georgina Lamb

The author wishes to express his gratitude
to the following for their support, without whom
The Frontline could not have been written:

Matthew Dunster, Dominic Dromgoole,
Leah Schmidt, Kirsten Foster

And massive love to the inner circle:

Zawe (inspiration beyond language and limits),
Sean, Elmo, Leomi, Ana, Lila, baby MJ, Jo Martin,
Tom Cowley, Dave Mafe and family, Michel Etienne,
Jeanine, Epiphany, Malo, Celia and all at WAC

*This text went to press before rehearsals had ended,
so may differ slightly from the play as performed*

Characters

Beth
Violet
Erkenwald
Ragdale
Donna
Mahmoud
Miruts
Marcus
Mordechai Thurrock
Salim
Benny
Jimmy
Seamus
Kurt
Polish Jodie
Casey
Elliot
Cockburn
Carlton
Val
Jayson
Roderique
Babydoll

THE FRONTLINE

Act One

A broad street, with a large London Underground
station flanked by the door to the 'fantasy bar', neon-lit,
with stairs running down to the basement.
    On the other side of the station is a phone booth.
    Further up to the right of the station is a cash machine.
    Various junkies and freaks mill about in various states
of intoxication.

Song
    We swagger and strut
    With broken bones
    We rob and steal
    We're the Invisible Ones
    We gettin high
    Till our eyes pop out
    And you ask us why
    We always scream and shout
    Invisible
    Invisible
    We're desperate and we're invisible
    Invisible
    Invisible
    But you still don't hear us though

Beth comes on with her troupe of Christians and sets
up her corner.

Beth
    Jesus
    Gave me water
    Jesus

Gave me water
Jesus gave me water
I wanna let his praises swell
Jesus gave me water
Jesus gave me water
Jesus gave me water
And it was not from the well

There was a woman from Sumeria
Who came to fetch some water
There she met a stranger
Who did a story tell
That a woman dropped her pitcher
Her reck'ning was made richer
From the water he gave her and it was not in the well
Yes, he gave her water
Jesus gave her water
Jesus gave her water
And I wanna let his praises swell

Jesus gave her water
He gave that woman water
He gave her living loving lasting water
And it was not from the well
Well, on that woman he had pity
She ran back to the city
Crying glory hallelujah
And did his wonders tell
She left my saviour singing
She came to him bringing
The time she had the water Lord
And it was not from the well

Beth preaches into a megaphone.
    *Violet enters. Thirties, very beautiful, but you
wouldn't want to piss her off.*

I was a sinner! I was a hopeless heartless dishonest sinner!

Christians Uh huh!

Beth I let other people abuse me!

Christians Yesss!

Violet Beautiful beautiful beautiful girls naked and unashamed!

Beth I let others misuse me! Yes I did, Lord!

Violet Wanna ease your sorrows and dissolve your dissatisfaction.

Erkenwald Get your lovely sausages sizzlin spicy sausages uhhh!

Beth Sought solace in chemical alleviation!

Christians Yes!

Erkenwald Sizzlin hot spicy sozzziiieeezzz huh!

Beth Sought comfort / in my appetite for sensation! Lost my soul, lost my love to lust and desire and destruction!

Violet (*overlapping from 'Sought comfort'*) Girls from all over the world all in the one spot dying to take off all their clothes and dance an American-style lapdance juss for you!

Erkenwald Sausage in a bun, lovely sausage in a bun!

Beth I had no idea that I was a child of the creator!

Violet Juss because you look so hot, juss cause they love to do it!

Beth I could not find the love in my heart!

Violet Only fifteen pound a dance. Fifteen pound a dance, ladies and gentlemen.

Beth Degradation was my daily ritual!

Ragdale, a neatly dressed, dapper man in his late
sixties, approaches Violet.

Violet Don't want trouble from you tonight, mister.

Beth Addiction was my daily ritual!

Violet Understand? Got the hump and I ain't got the patience.

Ragdale I knew you'd come.

Violet Not tonight, old man, I mean it.

Beth Drugs was my religion!

Christians Yes!

Ragdale My beautiful beautiful beautiful daughter –

Erkenwald Getchour sozziees!

Violet Fuck off!

Beth Deviance was my religion!

Ragdale My flower –

Violet Shut up!

Erkenwald Sizzlin spicy sausaaage huh!

Beth Decadent sexuality was my religion!

Donna, a London Underground worker in a yellow
bib and a hard hat, emerges from the tube entrance.

Erkenwald With the oniooonnnzzzz huh!

Ragdale My child –

Beth Oblivion was my religion!

Ragdale My heart –

Erkenwald Without the oniooonnnzzz huh!

6

Ragdale My love –

Beth And lemme tell yuh sumthin, people!

Violet Fuckin earache every night!

Beth I was an apostle of dissipated living until I found the Lord!

Violet Fuckin him in one ear and Mary fuckin Magdalene in the other!

Beth I been down!

Donna Oh, do leave off, love.

Erkenwald Hot dog with ketchuuuppp huh!

Christians Yes!

Ragdale It will take time, I know.

Erkenwald Hot dog wi no ketchuuuppp huh!

Mahmoud wheels on with his cart.

Mahmoud I have Qorma Alou-Bokhara, I have Afghan cooking very delicious for you!

Ragdale I understand.

Mahmoud Qorma from sour plums delicious.

Ragdale The experts said you'd find this part difficult.

Violet I'm warning you . . .

Beth Oh, you frail imperfect sinners!

Ragdale I love you –

Beth I know because I am you!

Ragdale You are my life.

Beth And I love you like the sun coming up!

Ragdale I'm waiting, darling.

Beth And Jesus has given me a gift to share with you!

Ragdale I'm waiting for you to see the truth.

Donna Are you mad? What do they call him? The Father, right? Everybody looking for a daddy to tuck them in at night. I dunno 'bout you, but I don't need a dad / and I never have. I'm both mother-father to my own self, mate, trust. Not some made-up daddy living up in the clouds. Thass juss keepin y'self an infant.

Beth (*overlapping from 'I don't need a dad'*) He wants me to gather you to him, like corn in the fields –

Ragdale You can cut me, punch me, hurt me and I won't forsake you. Not now that I've found you again.

Violet Old man, you really are dicing with death if you mess me about too much tonight . . .

Mahmoud Don't buy from the smelly hot dog man, his food is disease.

Ragdale opens up a dusty old photograph album.

Ragdale In this photograph you are small and you are running towards me as I open the door of our home.

Beth Jesus wants / to put his lips to your imperfections and blow them into dust.

Donna (*overlapping from 'Jesus wants'*) You running round believin in summink that can't be proved and you deaf to all objective reason –

Erkenwald Leave off, Mahmoud.

Donna Next thing you be believin in WMD or Stockwell police.

Erkenwald Don't try / and undermine me and my food!

Miruts Hashandweedhashandweed . . .

Ragdale (*overlapping from 'Don't try'*) You tell me you love me and your little arms stretch as wide as they could to show me how much . . .

Beth I can save you people –

Ragdale You strain your whole body, your whole face to show me the love you feel . . .

Beth I can! I can save you!

Enter Marcus. Big guy, in his thirties, in a suit. A bouncer at the strip joint.

Mahmoud This man is a serial killer!

Marcus There's some sorta fire down the street a ways.

Mahmoud This man is a pervert!

Marcus I think iss the Music Machine . . .

Erkenwald I'm gonna stick / you in one a' my hot dogs tonight if you don't shut up.

Marcus (*overlapping from 'stick'*) I don't want any dramas out of you tonight, old timer. Put your photo album away and behave y'self.

Mahmoud See?! See! All the street hear him! / He cook human flesh! This man not right!

Donna (*overlapping from 'hear him'*) You are babblin dangerous ancient / primitive nonsense and your ideas are enslaving countless human people.

Beth (*overlapping from 'ancient'*) He wants me to harvest you and make you healed, O beautiful children!

Christians Yes, Lord!

Ragdale In the spring, you pick me rocks from the park, and twigs, you paint them gold and purple and wrap them up and give them to me.

Marcus Hear what I said? No more drama.

Erkenwald Iss your food that smells like a mass grave, Mahmoud.

Violet You're late.

Mahmoud How you could bring up mass grave to me?

Ragdale And I say, 'What's this, little plumface?' and you say –

Erkenwald Fuck off!

Violet Stupid fantasist!

Ragdale You say it is your heart.

Mahmoud You bring up mass grave to Afghan man!

Ragdale And here's a snap of you on the beach –

Violet Old man!

Enter Miruts, perhaps as old as twenty, Ethiopian.

Miruts Hashandweedhashandweed . . .

Mordechai Thurrock Hi, I'm just leaving a message for Cressida Whitlock-Meadows regarding my one-man show at the Ephemera Theatre, and very much hoping to, ah, entice you down . . . / It's a fascinating historical piece, well, that's not strictly accurate, it's a piece of drama first and foremost, with a historical aspect to it . . . It's called *Sickert*, and it's about the dark mysterious figure of Walter Sickert, the influential Impressionist painter who started out, like me, as an actor in Sir Henry Irving's company, perhaps you remember seeing my college showcase in the Sir Henry Irving Studio in Bloomsbury.

Mahmoud (*overlapping from 'entice you down'*) Your mother is a mass grave!

Marcus If you go downstairs, then he can't bother you.

Erkenwald I'll rip your lungs out and stick 'em on the doner pole in a minute!

Violet Don't wanna go downstairs. Too hot down there.

Miruts Hashandweedhashandweed . . .

Beth I been down so low that my backside been scorched by the flames of hellfire!

Donna Why you can only be good cause some gigantic man in the sky tell you to be good, why can't you be good juss cause iss good to be good?

Marcus You won't make much money up here.

Donna Whasamatter, you gotta be told what to think?

Miruts Hashandweedhashandweedhashandweed . . .

Beth I used to let men do things to me that no man should do!

Donna Mental subjugation!

Violet Naked gyal wanna sit pon ya lap!

Beth No man should do!

Violet Man, I'm dyin out here, y'know that?

Donna I ain't gotta be told what to think.

Marcus It'll pick up.

Beth I been torn apart, chewed up and spat out by street life!

Violet Where's Bigboss? He's gonna shit thunder when he sees iss this quiet.

Marcus Bigboss ain't gona shit thunder.

Donna Lies being spun to keep us in a state of childish fear and unquestioning obedience.

Salim Skunk weed right here! Heavenly heavenly skunk make you forget your own name –

Beth There's no part of that life that I don't know!

Salim One puff you forget your own name, bredren, One puff and you can talk to your ancestors!

Beth I lived more like rat / than human woman!

Salim Skunk weed right heeeerre!

Beth So far from God's grace did I descend! So far from / the elegance of the human heart and spirit!

Miruts (*overlapping from 'So far from'*) Hashandweed hashandweedandhashandweed . . .

Benny and Jimmy come on.

Benny (*overlapping from 'rat'*) No, the thing about it is, I love the old fella but he juss wants to put the chains on me, y'know? I can't breath in that flat, I can't relax in that flat, I can't sing, I can't boogie –

Miruts Oy! Oy, fassyhole! I toldjuh already 'bout haunting these ends, man, and now I find you boldface under my neon just feeling you can shott and run up your lip like you somebody . . .

Jimmy Well, you know my feelings on the whole thing.

Salim Shutchour mouth!

Beth I took my dinner from the bottom of a garbage can!

Miruts Whynchou try and make me, weakheart?

Jimmy The guy's too old and clapped out, ain't no way thass gonna work.

Miruts I beg! Put you hands on me!

Beth I lay down with men and let them do their nastiness to me to separate / them from their money!

Violet (*overlapping from 'separate'*) Naked girls writhing / and gyrating!

Miruts (*overlapping from 'writhing'*) Be the last thing / you do!

Salim (*overlapping from 'last thing'*) Is who the fuck you think you're dealing wiv, mate?!

Benny Yeah, but you got ulterior motive, beautiful.

Miruts Who I'm dealing?

Beth But my life was still transformed . . . /

Miruts Who I'm dealing with?

Jimmy (*overlapping from 'transformed'*) I don't!

Beth I saw my reflection in the window and I leapt back in horror!

Jimmy I swear down!

Benny Don't lie, Jimmy, I know you got a thing for me!

Miruts You the only one I'm looking dead in the eye . . .

Jimmy I juss wanna be your friend and I juss wanna sing with you and I juss want you to be happy.

Beth A feral apparition! My hair was / falling from its roots upon my head!

Benny Methinks the lady doth protest too much.

Beth I was a fright!

Salim (*overlapping from 'my hair was'*) I find you think you talkin to a woman or somesuch and I don't much care for your tone, fassyhole.

Jimmy Shut up, Jimmy, you too neurotic for my tastes.

Miruts Bring it if you feelin bad.

Beth Hollow eyes!

Jimmy Iss juss a strickly musical romance, OK?

Salim You don't know who you're dealing wiv, mate.

Beth Sunken cheeks!

Salim I'll bring the thunder down from the sky to strike your ass . . .

Benny We'll see . . . /

Beth Teeth chipped like tombstones. A Moko Jumbie! A Zombie Woman!

Miruts (*overlapping from 'We'll see'*) You best be movin from this here vicinity or me and my soldiers gonna roll right through your ribcage juss like we do to your mother in Mogadishu.

Jimmy Iss the voice I desire, not the penis.

Beth And lemme tell yuh people / I clapped my eyes upon this terrible sight and I fell down to my knees then and there!

Salim (*overlapping from 'people'*) You wanna bring up Mogadishu? I was keepin a lid on things and you wanna bring up what you stinkin Ethiopian bastards / are doin in Mogadishu!

Benny (*overlapping from 'bastards'*) Yuh promise?

14

Beth And all the / traffic and the junkie zombies and the degenerate sodomites giving me a swerve, me wiv my hands clasped together!

Jimmy (*overlapping from 'And all the'*) Cross my heart, Benny.

Beth I arxed Jesus to enter my heart!

Benny Cause I can't take the complexity right now, alright?

Miruts Oh, what, struck a nerve, fassyhole?

Benny This whole thing with Seamus got me didgy and I juss need a friend.

Christians Jesus!

Beth Begged him to enter my heart!

Salim I'm gonna be feedin you your heart by the end of this night, / you stinkin Ethiopian communist bastards, you ain't even got the stamina to run your own county, you gotta pull in the Russians and Cubans and hide behind they skirts juss so you can see off the mighty Somalian forces, but we coming for you, little man, we comin for you, don't you worry 'bout dat!

Christians Jesus!

Beth Begged him to warm me! /

Benny *and* **Jimmy** (*sing, overlapping from 'this night'*)
    We got so much style and fascinating lyrics
    Musical biscuit
    Open up to hear it
    Cause we got magic
    Cause we got magic
    Elegance and charisma
    Like skunk weed in a Rizla

Style and fascination
Wanna pull my train up to your station
I'm your final destination
Magic and charisma

Miruts (*overlapping from 'Begged him to warm me'*) If you care so much about your home town, whyncha go back there and join up some rebel bullshit militia steada stinkin up this city here –

Enter Seamus.

Seamus (*to Benny*) I knew I'd find you here.

Christians Jesus!

Benny Oh, here we go . . .

Beth Begged him to hold me!

Seamus I want your stuff out by tonight.

Salim Ethiopia ain't got no bizness rolling in their frickin commie Russian-built rusty old tanks into my country!

Benny Where am I supposed to stay?

Christians Jesus!

Seamus (*a look to Jimmy*) I'm sure you'll have no problem finding somewhere to stay.

Miruts If iss your country, what you doin / selling ten bags of oregano to Japanese tourists round here?

Beth (*overlapping from 'doin'*) Begged him to cleanse me and purify my soul!

Jimmy I ain't got room for him, my mum'll kill me.

Seamus Is this what you do, make a move on a fella that doesn't belong to you?

Christians Jesus!

Benny Belong to you?

Salim Rrrrr! A gun! I'm a get me a gun!

Benny Belong to you?

Beth Purge me of the drugs!

Benny Thass your whole problem!

Miruts Ga ahead! I'll lend you a bullet!

Benny I ain't some trinket!

Salim I'm telling you, you little prick!

Beth Purge me of the alcohol!

Salim Your life is ebbing away! Tonight, you gonna die.

Erkenwald (*to audience*) He does die tonight, you'll see.

Benny And the days when you could own a human being done two hundred years back.

Miruts Your government asked us to come and save you from these lunatics runnin amok in your country –

Benny This what this is? You got a little exoticist slave-master thing in your mind?

Seamus That is so beneath you.

Beth Purge me of the sexual disgrace!

Benny I chose you! You ain't bought me!

Salim Them rebel fellas is brave fellas.

Benny You ain't rescued me!

Salim They the best chance we got.

Seamus Then stick around out here among this, this . . .

Beth And what do you think Jesus did for me?

Seamus This scum!

Miruts Best chance for what?

Beth My people, what do you think the Lord did for me?

Miruts Sharia law?

Seamus If you can't see what I've given you and the life / I'm trying to show you that's out there, then –

Miruts Juss what Somalia needs!

Beth (*overlapping from 'the life'*) He filled me my heart and healed my soul and flooded my being with awe and love till it hurt me to hold it!

Seamus Then I guess it juss was never a real thing.

Salim Those rebels are good Muslim like me.

Christians Yes, Lord! /

Miruts Muslim?

Beth He washed me clean!

Seamus (*overlapping from 'Yes, Lord'*) And I guess I juss been used like my friends warned me you would.

Miruts You're a Muslim now?

Beth He threshed me till I was a husk!

Miruts What part of you is Muslim?

Benny That is it!

Salim I am Muslim! /

Benny THAT IS IT!

Beth He made me naked and newborn and able to see and to love and progress!

Miruts (*overlapping from 'He made me'*) You ain't no Muslim! I know Muslim! My little shop on the corner, thass Jamal and his brother from Chechnya, thass real Muslim! Nice people! Lemme have a little tick if I'm short for a pack a' dem superthin kingsize Rizla! Sensitive people! Islam is peace and knowledge and mathematics –

Salim Shut up!

Benny (*overlapping from 'I am Muslim'*) You the one thass using me, you suckin up my youth and my vitality, you treatin me like some sorta pet project and you ain't even ever heard me singin not once, not to one single gig not when I'm noodlin on the piano –

Seamus My piano –

Benny You got no int'rest in my music or me who I am!

Benny leaves.

Seamus Benny! Come back!

Miruts You ain't no Muslim, you about as Islamic as a bacon samwich.

Beth And I want to do that for you!

Jimmy He's right, Grandad, Benny got a talent for music and you ain't even hearin it.

Seamus Shut up!

Miruts And if you Muslim you don't drink or smoke –

Seamus What you telling me about my boyfriend for?

Miruts – and you definitely don't sell no skunk weed!

Jimmy 'Low it, man, I don't need this.

Jimmy leaves.

Seamus Bennnnyyyy!!

An enormous fight breaks out between twenty Somalian youths and twenty Ethiopian youths. Seamus is in the crossfire but Donna pulls him to safety.

Beth (*overlapping the fight*) I want to deliver you from the needle and the crack pipe and the bottle and skunk weed spliff thass twistin up you minds! Take my hands and we can move towards the effervescence of his presence!

If you come wiv me and come to Jesus we can transform ourselves, and have a world where we can trust our young people, our children, not to destroy and we can trust our elders not to abuse!

Universal love for all people, my people, yes –

The fight escalates till the sound of sirens disperses the youths.

Erkenwald Oh yes, what a thrill, what a drama! Poor little lost lambs gotta fight each other, and you know why they doin that? It ain't for pride, it ain't for turf, and it certainly ain't for their shaky grasp of geopolitics . . . They fighting each other juss so they can touch each other, so they can contact each other. If human beings don't get physical contact, thass when they start to bend double under the weight of their own loneliness. They're juss lonely li'l hooligan scumbag basstads really, thass all.

Beth (*sings*)
    Jesus
    Come down to heal me
    Jesus
    Come down to claim me
    Jesus
    Come down to release me
    Jesus
    Come down to name me
    Take me

Claim me
Heal me
Release me
Burn me
And make me yours

Erkenwald Yuh hear all thing the God-botherer was
blathering? Yuh wanna know whass wrong wiv all that?
She don't know what the meaning of the word love is.
She's is labouring under a common misconception. She
thinks love is some light from the sky fill yuh body up
and warm yuh like Ready Brek. And thass not what it is.
Love is a verb. Not a feeling. Iss a verb. And verb is
word to describe action. Iss a doing word. Love is not
something yuh feel. Love is sumthing yuh *do*. And thass
whass wrong wiv us all, we looking to be feelin when we
need to be *doin*. Makes sense? Man, life can get all up
in your ass, so you better work it out. Before iss all dust
and regret.

Mordechai Thurrock Hi, I'm leaving a message again
for Cressida Whitlock-Meadows, ah, having some
trouble with my mobile for some reason, I just wanted
to make sure you had the times of the show, we run at
seven-thirty p.m. sharp nightly, that's seven-thirty p.m.,
tickets are twelve English pounds only.

Mahmoud Qoooorrmaaaaa!!

Seamus Thank you, miss, that was a close one.

Kurt Beth? You OK? You didn't get hurt?

Donna Them boys get worse each night.

Beth Nah, I'm cool.

Seamus I was just out here talkin with –

Donna Your boyfriend, I know –

Mordechai Thurrock But, uh, I would be happy to organise a complimentary for you if you call me at the theatre –

Marcus gets out a battered old detective book. He settles himself down and gets into reading.

Violet Don't get out that same blasted book, Marcus.

Donna (*to Seamus*) He'll come back.

Kurt That was . . . that was insane. Like some sorta . . .

Seamus What?

Beth Some sorta visitation.

Violet Marcus, stop reading.

Donna He'll come back.

Mordechai Thurrock And, actually, uh, if you can't make it for seven-thirty, say, you're caught up with the office, what-have-you, then I could arrange for the curtain to go up slightly later –

Seamus Why do you think you can talk to me about my private, uh, uh – my private things?

Violet Bleeding book-readers . . .

Marcus It keeps me calm to read after all this tumult.

Donna I don't mean to speak outta turn, but I saw you and your young man at *The Battle of Algiers* last Sunday –

Violet Marcus!

Seamus *Battle of Algiers?*

Kurt Heh. A plague of frogs or some shi— er, some mess.

Seamus You were there?

22

Beth You didn't get hurt, did you?

Donna Wicked, isn't it?

Mordechai Thurrock And, also, the show is very short, it runs at just over ninety minutes –

Seamus You like Pontecorvo?

Kurt You know you doing well, Beth, being out here.

Donna Why wouldn't I?

Mordechai Thurrock So you'll be out in time to catch a cocktail with me, before going home.

Donna You tryna fit me in sorta box?

Beth I wanted to do it and I'm glad that I did.

Seamus No, I –

Beth Anybody can save a soul up in Hampstead, thass small ting –

Donna Juss cos I work for London Underground don't mean I'm ignorant.

Beth It takes a dedicated soldier for the Lord to do it here.

Seamus No, I didn't mean to, uh –

Violet Marcus, stop reading!

Beth Here among / the destitution.

Donna 'S juss you look like a thoughtful individual thass all, the young fella looks to me like he loves you, I could see that even at the Pontecorvo.

Marcus (*overlapping from 'Here among'*) What am I s'posed to do? Nobody here. Nothing to do.

Seamus Presumptuous but kind of intriguing.

Violet Ev'ry night. You have any idea how boring it is to talk to someone who's reading a book?

Mordechai Thurrock Hi, Cressida, Mordechai here – I really wouldn't keep calling you if it wasn't for my passionate excitement about the project –

Seamus This place is insane.

Donna Cheaper than the movies.

Mordechai Thurrock There really is some extraordinary theatre happening down here.

Seamus Y'not wrong.

Pause.

Violet You are such an irritatin person for me, Marcus.

Marcus starts to read.

Mordechai Thurrock Was Walter Sickert the actual Jack the Ripper of legendary Victorian times?

Kurt I can't imagine what it's like, coming to this spot again . . .

Mordechai Thurrock The painting shows a man wringing his hands in torment, his head bowed in enormous guilt.

Beth I can handle it.

Mordechai Thurrock He is sitting on the end of a bed . . . On the bed is the lifeless form of a murdered prostitute. Does his mysterious painting, *The Camden Town Murder*, hold the key to one of the enduring and fascinating mysteries of all times?

Kurt The associations –

Mordechai Thurrock Was it Sickert's confession?

Kurt – the temptations . . .

24

Mordechai Thurrock Or was he an unwilling accomplice in covering up the crime for Prince Albert, dangerously deranged by genital syphilis?

Kurt Girl, you got your head right up in the lion's mouth . . . I admire you and I'm right by your side.

Mordechai Thurrock The only way to find out is to come to the Ephemera Theatre, above The Sussex pub –

Beth Likewise, lover.

Mordechai Thurrock – and catch rising young star Mordechai Thurrock's brilliantly inventive and terrifying new play *Sickert*.

Kurt Come on, lover, less go home and cuddle.

Beth I'm gonna stick around here and talk to some a' these people . . . The maddest thing is they ain't even the same guys I used to see . . . The turnover rate round here is insane . . .

Mordechai goes over to Mahmoud.

Mordechai Thurrock Have you got any ten pence pieces?

Mahmoud No! Fuck off.

Kurt You can't save them all, beautiful.

Beth You gotta try.

Kurt I don't like it out here . . . Less go home . . .

Beth I'm staying.

Mordechai goes to Erkenwald.

Mordechai Thurrock Have you got any ten pence pieces? I need change for the phone.

Kurt Beth . . . Roderique might still be floating round these ends.

Erkenwald How comes you don't have a mobile?

Beth Nah . . . I would know . . .

Mordechai Thurrock Do you have any change?

Kurt How would you know?

Erkenwald I need my change for my customers.

Beth A connection like that . . . Things we used to do to each other and to others . . . I'd feel his presence . . .

Erkenwald Buy something from me and I'll give you change for the phone.

Kurt I ain't really all that easy about this still, Beth . . .

Mordechai Thurrock You only sell hot dogs. I'm an ethical vegan.

Beth Kurt . . . You think I'd go back to those ways?

Erkenwald Oh, for fuck's sakes . . .

Beth You think I'd forsake what we got growing between us?

Erkenwald Man was born a hunter, you foolish boy.

Kurt I think about him sometimes and I wonder what I'd do if I met him . . .

Erkenwald Why do you think we have canine teeth?

Kurt If I could be Christian and extend a hand to him after all the things you told me he put you through . . .

Erkenwald It wasn't for ripping apart tofu.

Kurt And the truth is, I don't know.

Beth Lover . . . Roderique is in my past and you are in my future.

Erkenwald Thass why you so pallid and sallow, you little slip a' grease, look atcha.

Beth Kurt . . . I love you like a last chance.

A Christian comes running up.

Christian Kurt . . . Come . . .

Mordechai Thurrock I don't actually choose to discuss this with you.

Kurt Catch your breath, man, whass wrong widjuh?

Christian Someone's done us over . . .

Erkenwald Why not? Don't I have a point?

Kurt What?

Christians The mission. Someone set it on fire . . . The place looks . . .

Kurt Have they taken much?

Donna Oy, mate.

Christian Come.

Donna You been done over?

Kurt Beth . . .

Beth I'm needed here.

Kurt Beth . . .

Beth You're needed there.

Kurt leaves with the Christians.

Donna Lemme help.

Donna exits, following Kurt. Beth remains.
Seamus nearly follows, but Polish Jodie comes on.

Polish Jodie (*in Polish*) Mister, take me to Richard right now! I know you know where he is! Take me there! Take me to drugs now!

Seamus Uh . . . Sorry, I –

Polish Jodie (*in Polish*) Please! Please! I'm in so much pain . . .

Polish Jodie bursts into tears and holds on to Seamus. Seamus, not knowing what to do, holds her back, if at a little distance.

Mordechai Thurrock I'm sorry, but I just won't eat meat.

Erkenwald I'm sorry, but I juss don't give change unless you buy summink.

Mordechai huffs and puffs. Then hands over a grubby five-pound note.

Marcus Whass 'relentless' mean?

Violet Whass the context?

Marcus 'He grabbed Jack by his lapel with his left hand. His right hand smashed into his face relentlessly.'

Erkenwald Now do you want onions with that?

Violet It means he hit him a lotta times, Marcus.

Marcus Good. This guy in this book, right –

Violet How comes you've never asked me out?

Mordechai Thurrock I don't want the bloody thing at all!

Erkenwald Well, you're havin it, so you might as well have onions!

Marcus sighs and puts down his book.

Violet I ain't exactly a dog.

Pause.

I said I ain't exactly a dog.

Pause.

Ain't doing bad for three kids. Li'l bit of wear and tear here and there, but nothing major . . . Still make my living with my looks. How comes you never asked me out?

Marcus Because you're relentless.

Violet Think you're smart cause you stay fully clothed.

Marcus I don't think I'm smart, Violet.

Marcus returns to his book.

Violet Too tall to be a bouncer anyway. Best bouncers are the little squat ones, like bulldogs. Low centre of gravity, y'see. Can't push 'em over so easily. You widjour long self. Strong wind'd knock you on your arse.

Ragdale And here's a picture of your sonogram –

Violet Shut up.

Marcus Just for a while, eh, Captain? Enough.

Ragdale I can wait as long as I have breath in my body.

Mordechai Thurrock Hi Cressida, it's Mordechai Thurrock here again. Listen, I just had an unusual kooky idea – if you're having trouble making the time to see the show – wait for it – why don't I bring the show to where you are?

Violet What you reading for, Marcus?

Marcus I'm tryina make my thoughts more better than what they are and to do that you need to read.

Ragdale The songs we sang together . . .

Mordechai Thurrock I've designed the set, and it can be packed up into a case and brought to your office. I could run it for you there!

Ragdale We would play / pittterpat clapping game and you'd scold me for every mistake.

Violet (*overlapping from 'We would play'*) I'm gonna snatch that book out of your hands and tear it to fuck before the night's out.

Mordechai Thurrock What do you think? Unconventional, I know.

Marcus puts down the book.

Marcus Why's it when you wanna grow, there's always people wanna hold you back?

Mordechai Thurrock Drop me a line at the theatre and let's make it happen.

Marcus They see this book like iss some sorta reproach. Iss juss . . . nutrition. It ain't a reproach.

Ragdale And sometimes we would –

Violet Shut up. Whass a reproach?

Marcus Like I'm telling you off for not being good enough.

Violet Fuckin better not be saying that. I'm more than good enough for you, truss.

Marcus Lemme read my book, Vi.

Enter Casey, thirties.

Casey Nightmare journey, been chuckin up all day at the bar, then there's some sorta fire on the tube, we all gotta get out and walk the tracks and get on a rail replacement bus and there's this dirty smelly fella gets his cock out in

30

the upper deck, all these people tryina pretend they ain't starin at a fair-size pecker in their boat and me thinking anyhow he comes near me with that thing he's gonna lose it, but then he drapes it over this woman's Jilly Cooper like iss a bookmark and she screams and freaks out and starts hitting him in his cock with the Jilly Cooper and then some fool pulls the emergency cord and so I had to get off the bus and catch a cab, ended up costing me a fortune and I didn't have money so the cabbie's coming for a free dance when he gets off work around three a.m. Any a youse lot seen Jayson?

Ragdale Oh, you've come at last . . .

Casey What?

Ragdale Now we can repair the rift.

Casey I ain't got changed yet, old man. Lemme get into my dress and then we'll repair the rift.

Ragdale I've had nights when I thought you were lost for ever, but a tiny little whisper in me just persisted, persisted –

Casey What the fuck you chattin about? You starting up on this bollox again and I ain't even got in my work clothes?

Ragdale We were so close when you were little, you idolised me, and I know I made mistakes, and I'm willing to examine that like the experts said I should –

Casey Mate? I don't wanna be rude, right . . . But if you keep talking to me as if you're a crazy person, then watch me when I grips up your actual throat.

Marcus Alright, Casey . . . He don't mean no harm . . . He's juss a li'l cracked, y'know? No need for the vitriolics . . .

Casey Nah. I don't like that kinda talk. He needs to learn. Coming out here every night saying he's my dad. I have a perfectly good father of my own and I'm not in the market for another one. I'm getting changed. Keep this freak away from me.

Violet Come on, Casey. Less raid the bar while iss quiet. Leave the old man to his madness –

Casey You heard from Jayson today?

Seamus (*to Polish Jodie*) Uh, love . . . could you let me go now? It's going to be alright . . .

Polish Jodie (*in Polish*) Fuck off! Idiot! Wanker! Fuckin weak man! The world is full of spineless men who can't make decisions!

Polish Jodie storms off.
Ragdale sees Beth.

Ragdale Ah! There! Oh! Yesss . . . The age is right, oh!

Violet I think he passed early.

Beth Hello, sir, are you ready to make Jesus Christ your personal saviour?

Casey He's keeping summink from me.

Ragdale Do you know the joy I'm getting from having found you?

Beth Er . . . That's . . . wonderful, sir.

Casey If Jayson's fightin again, I'll kill him . . .

Ragdale And it's not beyond repair.

Marcus Nah. He's working at the garage.

Casey You really can't lie at all, can you, Marcus?

Marcus What?

Ragdale You and I can put the past behind us.

Casey You look like you're five years old.

Marcus What?

Violet and Casey exit into the strip club.

Ragdale And we can move on together and put the past behind us.

Beth Sir?

Ragdale opens up his photo album.
  Enter Elliot, sixteen, belligerently talking into his mobile.

Ragdale Here's a picture of you with your bottle to your mouth, stubbornly drinking,

Elliot Yeah, Richard, I'm at the spot.

Ragdale I see your tiny fist clutching hold of your ear as you drink –

Elliot So who's the br'er I gotta find?

Ragdale – fighting off sleep because you just want to see an' hear the whole world in one gulp –

Elliot He ain't here.

Ragdale – till it overwhelms you and you sigh and your eyes droop one at a time and I pluck the bottle from your lips and scoop you up in my arms and I carry you off –

Elliot Nope, no one looking like that is here.

Ragdale You smell of milk and cotton, you smell of hope.

Beth Whoa . . .

Elliot (*to Ragdale*) Oy, mate, you see an oldish looking geeza round here with a two-tone suit on?

Ragdale I'm talking to my daughter.

Elliot (*into phone*) Richard, I'll call yuh back. Whatchou say to me?

Ragdale I am having a very difficult and sensitive conversation with my daughter.

Elliot You best start being polite to me cause I got some buttons on me you don't wanna be pushin, mate. I will ruin the rest of your life if you don't start talking to me like I'm an adult, y'understand, before I cave in your whole skull with my fists.

Ragdale Young ruffians like you hold no fear for me. You're talking to a man who escaped from Colditz.

Elliot Well, escape from here.

Beth Come on . . . Can't you see he's an elder?

Elliot Now you wanna get involved. Lissen, Sister of Mercy, or whatever the fuck you call y'self now, I seen you on this corner talking 'bout Jesus this and Jesus that, givin the whole block a bleeding headache widdat nonsense. Stop pretending you summink that you not, I know your scummy true self, I used to see you widjour junkie romance Roderique skulking round the canal looking for a purse to snatch and I can tell from one good look in those eyes that you still hunger to party, so when you ready I'm juss on this corner and you and me can get high and then I'll slip it to you nice and slow and deep cause I'm sixteen and a half years old and you ain't never had no loving like it I should be in the Olympics with what I got, this Weapon of Ass Destruction can go all night and I can climax three times without going soft and iss a real big one but iss a pretty one also – wanna see it?

Miruts Oy, Elliot, I hear you and Richard is partnered up and makin some sabre-tooth manouevres out here, blud.

Elliot Don't watch me and Richard.

Violet goes over to Mahmoud.

Violet Yeah, gimme one a' dem Turkish coffee, please.

Miruts Ain't watchin nuffink but my own skinny self out here –

Mahmoud Afghan.

Miruts But thass some deep waters you swimmin in.

Violet What?

Miruts Richard don't ramp.

Mahmoud Afghan coffee.

Elliot What, are you in the fuckin Samaritans now or summink?

Miruts I'm juss sayin . . .

Violet Whatever.

Miruts That kinda commerce ain't like knockin out a little bit a' weed.

Violet Juss gimme some caffeine.

Miruts Thass . . . deep-sea deep.

Cockburn enters, forties.

Cockburn You the kid that Richard sent?

Elliot Yeah, thass me.

Cockburn You strike me as somewhat of a loose cannon to my way of thinking.

35

Elliot Don't you worry bout me, mister, I can handle my bizness, yeah? So whatchou got for us?

Cockburn This not some small piece of dried-up commersh, this is some expensive substance I'm putting in your care and I don't want you fuckin it up.

Miruts Hey, mate, the guy can handle it, and I'm on hand to make sure he does.

Cockburn Who the fuck is this?

Elliot This is nobody at all. (*To Miruts.*) Fuck off before I kill you.

Cockburn Is this a joke? I don't deal with his kind.

Miruts Oh, now I know you didn't juss say that. He didn't juss say that, did he?

Elliot Shut up and fuck off. You're distressin the sesh.

Cockburn Ain't got no ethics cause you're not really from here, got no loyalty to the place. How can you know how to conduct y'self? This is a different planet in terms of our values and our traditions . . .

Miruts Oh jeez . . . I gettin lessons in decorum from some busted-down cocaine dealer . . . You making me laugh, blood. You gonna teach me ethics?

Cockburn Iss different, we're Christians here.

Miruts Ethiopia the first country outside a' Israel to worship Christ, we in the Bible forty times, Tewahedo church been spreading Christian philosophy since the fourth century –

Mahmoud Tewahedo – comes from Arabic – one God.

Miruts – round about the time you English bastards was eating your own shit and pickin the lice outchour fur.

Cockburn grips him up.
  Miruts struggles with him.
  The Street protests.

Cockburn Donchou try and take me for a fool. I been
on these streets doing damage when your father was on
the boat dreamin 'bout housing benefits . . . Don't keep
talking to me . . .

Cockburn throws him against a wall.

Elliot Gwan old fella! Drop the hammer on him.

Cockburn grips up Elliot.

Cockburn You and your fuckin li'l hip-hop Tony Montana
bollocks is starting to grate on me, sunshine . . . Have
a look at my face . . . See the crow's feet? See the long
gums? See the grey hair on my head? See my scars?
I earnt them all . . . I ain't some li'l prick juss out his
nappies that you can freeze with a scowl. I am Paul
fuckin Muni, y'understand?

Violet Scuse me . . . This how you get your thrills,
gripsing up li'l defenceless children that can't fight back?
Big man like you. You should be ashamed, mate.

Marcus Violet . . .

Cockburn Looks like you one more lady gonna be
spending the night in A&E cause a' your big flapping
lips. Ain't you got a conscience, putting a burden on our
strugglin NHS? You come over here –

Violet I was born here!

Cockburn Here we go . . .

Violet We been here since Julius Caesar times! And the
NHS would collapse tomorrow if it wasn't for us, so move
y'self! Alla this place! The National Portrait Gallery!

We built it! Trafalgar Square! We built it! We built your schools, your prisons, your houses, your roads –

Seamus I think the Irish might have had something to do with that –

Violet This country kickin back and eating good cause we bust our spines gettin exploited and abused, so don't come around here and –

Cockburn I don't wanna hear your crap! If it wasn't for us, the whole world'd be speakin German –

Violet Oh Lord put a hand –! This obsession with World War Fuckin Two, iss like you lot ain't got fuck all to talk about, if that war meant so much to you then why you leave the ones who fought it and lived it, why them all in old people home sitting in their own piss? Huh? Oh, and yes, we was there too, the West Indians, the Africans and the Indians, we shed blood in that thing and all, and juss why is it you think that li'l six-year period makes up for hundreds of years of rape, murder, slavery and apartheid, ya fuckin ugly red-faced bag of prejudice? Four hundred years of it and you still can't say you're sorry!

Cockburn Sorry for what? For teaching you how to walk on two legs?

Violet Fuck off! You most probly ain't even English anyway! Less take a li'l DNA off you, eh? What we gonna find? You hundred-per-cent confident you pure breed Angle or Celtic? You most probly some sorta Danish Viking from when they rowed up the River Thames and took out your whole crew and claimed London for thesselves, the Danes kicked your arse in the one thousands and took the place over, the Germans kicked your arse and took the place over, the Romans, even the fuckin French kicked your arse cause youse lot can chuck it like

38

you're Jimmy the Fuckin Biscuit, but when it comes
down to it, you English juss can't fuckin fight!

Cockburn moves as if to strike her.
Violet pulls out a blade.
A huge commotion and kerfuffle involving all the
people.
Miruts steals Cockburn's package of cocaine. He
steals away, unseen by Cockburn.
The brawl subsides.

Cockburn Hold on . . . Hold on one little frickin second.
Where's my . . . where's my – where's my works?!

The rest of the Street shrug.

Who saw what happened to my works? Oy. Elliot, is it?
You nicked it?

Elliot Now why would I do that?

Cockburn Where's it? Right. That is it. Missus. You
with the knockers hangin out. Come here.

Violet If you gonna talk to me like that, I'll slice you a
new set a lips.

Cockburn moves surprisingly fast.
He disarms Violet and has her in a headlock.
He swiftly grabs a styrofoam cup of coffee from her.

Cockburn You gonna tell me what I need to know or
am I gonna pour this scalding hot coffee all over those
blowjob lips a yourn? Eh? That what you want? Be such
a shame to disfigure that prettiness, wouldn't it? Whassit
gonna be, sweetheart?

Ragdale knocks the coffee from Cockburn's hand.

Ragdale Unhand my daughter this instant!

Cockburn throws Violet roughly to the floor. She is
slightly concussed.

Cockburn bitch-slaps Ragdale, grabs his photo album and throws it into the pit.

My photographs! Don't touch them!

Ragdale scrambles after them, hugely distressed.

Cockburn Now who else wants to try it wimme? Eh? I've already got the ravin hump!

Erkenwald Eh, mate . . .

Erkenwald has advanced from behind his hot-dog stall with a large glinting cleaver.

(*Menacing.*) How would you like me to fix you up with a lovely hot dog with all the trimmings, pal? Eh?

Mahmoud (*menacing*) Or some lovely Qorma a Lou-Bokharma?

Mahmoud has advanced from his spot with a giant kebab skewer.

Erkenwald (*threatening*) Nice spot of mustard on the bun . . .

Cockburn looks at him.

Mahmoud (*threatening*) Cardamom and carmelizzzed onionszzz . . .

Cockburn looks at him.
They are both pretty close.

Erkenwald You sure, old fella?

Mahmoud Come on . . . One bite . . .

Erkenwald Can't tempt yuh?

Cockburn backs off.

Cockburn All right, you freaks . . . all right. But this is destruction you're bringin upon y'selves . . . You hear

about Fallujah? Thass whass coming for you . . .
Genocide for alla yuh . . . I can make one phone call and
turn this whole street into a moon crater . . . I'll burn
you and bury you and shit upon your bones . . . This is
juss gettin started. Freaks.

Cockburn exits.
Erkenwald and Mahmoud look at each other, warily,
grudgingly respectful.

Marcus Vi? You alright, darling?

Elliot Hey Miruts, you nutcase fool.

Violet Oh, it's darling now?

Elliot You best give him back his works or this whole
street gonna be stardust.

Violet You stand there and let some man do that to me!

Miruts I don't see how what I give or don't give has any
bearing on your wellbeing whatsoever.

Violet You muss juss not care 'bout me at all, thass what
you think a' me, / that I'm juss some tart that you can
watch getting abused then you go and fuck your own
bollox till they bleed.

Marcus Don't be like that, Vi –

Violet storms off.

Erkenwald (*to Marcus*) Hehheh . . .

Marcus Leave me alone, Erkenwald.

Elliot (*overlapping from 'thass what you think a' me'*)
See . . . Thass the thing . . . Thass why this country's
youth is going to shit . . . You lot ain't got no morality . . .
You fuckin it up for the rest of us . . . You giving youth
a bad name, juss when things cracking open for us, here
you come making us all look like lunatics . . .

41

Miruts Crackin open for you . . . Take a look . . . Ain't nothing cracking open for nobody on this corner . . . We're still scrabbling for scraps . . .

Elliot Well, lemme tell you it like this . . . If my name gets dragged into this . . . If Richard is displeased by any a' this . . . I'll come back for you and I'll put you in the ground myself . . . Ethiopian bastard.

Miruts Yeah, yeah . . . Go run and hide behind Richard's coat tails, ya baby.

Erkenwald 1690. King's Cross. Archaeologists find a woolly mammoth perfectly intact in the clay. A fuckin woolly mammoth! Shark bones been found in the River Thames. Not li'l stupid sharks with dopey faces but right hard bastard no-mercy sharks. And in the forest . . . Lions and tigers and bears, oh my . . . All been found in the clay you're standing on . . . What a time it must have been . . . I tell you one thing, pal . . . compared to these kids out here, I'd take my chances with the fuckin mammoth.

Mordechai Thurrock Hi, Cressida, Mordechai Thurrock here . . . I realised I haven't really identified myself, I gave you my card at my graduation showcase and we talked about Michael Chekhov, Kabuki and music hall for a while . . . I'm [young and blondish with greeny-blue eyes . . . I was the one my principal said had a sort of Peter O'Toole quality about me.] (*Or whatever the actor playing the part looks like.*)

> *Carlton comes on. Stops in horror when he sees Mordechai Thurrock in 'his' phone booth.*

Carlton Oy. Oy. Oy. Oy. Thass my home you're standing in, mate, juh mind tellin me what you're doin in there? Is that how you normally behave, mate? Thass fuckin anti-social, that is.

Mordechai Thurrock Don't come too close, you stink.

Carlton Thass rude –

Mordechai Thurrock Keep away. Keep away.

Carlton Mate, thass my sleeping bag and my rucksack, everyone here knows iss mine –

Mordechai Thurrock Further back.

Carlton Did no one stop you? Erkenwald!

Erkenwald Whadjuh want?

Carlton Didn't yuh tell this ponce that he was steppin into my home?

Erkenwald Hadn't seen you for a while, I was hopin you'd OD'd.

Carlton Fuckin hell! Is this how you treat your neighbour?

Erkenwald My real neighbours ain't thievin burglin smackheads like you, Carlton –

Carlton I've watched your cart when you went for a piss many a time, Erkenwald, don't chuck it!

Erkenwald I come back and you'd eaten the entire sozzies!

Carlton I was doing you a favour! The meat had gone off, if you'd sold them you'd a been closed down.

Erkenwald Juss cause you puked your guts out after eating seventeen sausages in one sitting don't mean the meat was bad, it juss means you're a junkie who's lost control of his appetite!

Carlton Mate . . . I need to go to bed now . . . Thass been my home for a many a month, iss got all my gear

43

in it and I keep it clean . . . Respect my privacy, yeah? Respect my privacy and piss off.

Mordechai Thurrock Don't touch me. I need to use the phone.

Carlton Mate . . . Iss after midnight, who is it you gotta speak to? Your dealer?

Mordechai Thurrock I'm using the phone. I suggest you make alternative arrangements for your accommodation.

Carlton Mate . . . I know I might not look like much to you, but once upon a time I was in the Royal Green Jackets, and even with my li'l problem habit, I'll still take you apart, mate. I might have lost a little bit of fitness to the needle and the spoon but I been living in a phone booth, what, you think I don't know how to fight my corner? Y' better step, mate.

Mordechai moves.
Carlton slides into the phone booth and proceeds to get a fix of heroin together and inject it into his arms.
Enter Val.

Val Elliot . . .

Elliot Oh fuckin hell . . .

Val Elliot, this is . . . This is unnatural.

Elliot Move from me.

Val Elliot . . .

Elliot Oh Jesus . . . I toldjuh already not to come down here, this place ain't for you, now move from here.

Val Elliot, this ain't right how you do. You gotta come back to how you was before.

Elliot This is how I've always been.

44

Val How am I s'posed to sleep when I know you down among the blades and vengeance? This is gonna kill me, / Elliot, my hair getting thin, my bones don't click right . . . I'm dyin causa alla this . . .

Elliot (*overlapping from 'This is gonna kill me'*) Mum . . . This ain't some martyrdom thing now, alright? Your illness ain't got nuttin to do wimme, you juss ill cause it gives you summink to focus on. Move.

Val I'm getting panicked and anxious and I'm feelin alone.

Elliot All your bleatin and palpitatin ain't nuttin to do wimme or my runnins.

Val Iss Richard's done this, innit? Where is he? That why you out here?

Elliot Oh Jesus . . .

Val I know that viper Richard's sucked you into all this, I know it.

Elliot I ain't even a little bit int'rested in your opinion bout Richard! You forfeited alla that when you decided you liked Valium more than motherhood. The Most High give you a gift of a child and you squandered it cause self-obsess and indulge your mind in torment, so don't come round here and tell me to cast aside the one rock-solid friend that I got! I wouldn't have even got through school without the man!

Val He's a murderer, he's taken lives and he's ain't even twenty.

Elliot SHUT UP! No more fuckin babblin. It stops now. You ain't been babblin when your sixteen-year-old son clearing up your rent arrears, have ya? And you carryin on like I ain't a man. You ain't even capable of holding

45

down a steady job cause you can't keep your hands from shakin –

Val I – I get nervous, son –

Elliot I'm going to see Richard and tell him how the drop gone sour. This corner is for scrappers and battlers. Not for weakhearts like you. When I get back, you best be far from here, tucked up and tranquilised, or I'm a get cross.

Elliot exits.
  Val frets, unsure whether to chase him.
  Ragdale emerges. He stops in shock.

Ragdale Ah! I knew I'd find you! Oh that face . . . Etched with tribulation, but still my little girl . . . And I am so, so, so, so sorry for all that happened when you –

Val Someone get him away, I'm gettin nervous.

Marcus Alright, alright . . . Come on, old-timer . . . Less got inside and get you a Horlicks or somesuch, alright?

Ragdale proffers his photo album.

Ragdale Look! Here's one of you asleep on the ferry back from Normandy, see how you have your hair in the same way even then . . .

Enter Polish Jodie, speaking into mobile phone.

Polish Jodie (*in Polish*) Can't find that freak Richard and I really need to get off my tits . . . Yeah, yeah, yeah . . . I'm trying . . . Bigboss isn't around either . . . I don't know . . .

Ragdale starts in shock, then takes off after her.

Ragdale This is more than I ever hoped for! My daughter, my love, my child, we can be together again!

46

Polish Jodie exits, pursued by Ragdale.
  Mordechai Thurrock returns.

Carlton Oh, hello . . . Little Lord Fauntleroy . . .

Mordechai Thurrock All the other phone booths don't
work any more and they stink of piss. Please . . . Please,
I'm sorry I was rude to you before . . . This is such an
important phone call I have to make –

Carlton Y'lucky I juss put some medicine in my veins
and I'm full of the milk of human kindness overflowing
through my blood . . .

*Pause. Mordechai Thurrock realises that Carlton isn't
going to move, so he leans awkwardly over him and
pumps the phone full of ten-pence pieces.*

Donna I remember you from the school cross the road.
You know, One-Eyed Bruce and all that lot from
Ravenscar.

Mordechai Thurrock Hi, Cressida, just a little bit more
background on the show.

Miruts Why you so int'rested in who I know? You don't
know me.

Mordechai Thurrock It begins with Joseph Sickert,
Walter's illegitimate love child, played by myself –

Donna You always so rude when pretty girls lyrix you
on road?

Mordechai Thurrock – confronting Sickert on his
deathbed . . .

Donna You must be all super-scared from all this
shenanigans.

Mordechai Thurrock Then Walter, also played by me, as
he realises his life is ending, makes his confession . . .

Miruts Got a better look at you now . . . You go drinkin in that spot juss off Belmont.

Mordechai Thurrock 'Degas had advised me to escape the tyranny of nature . . . but when your nature is as fatal as my nature, escape becomes impossible.'

Donna Thass me. I usually go with Tina and them.

Mordechai Thurrock Then we see Sickert's sister Helena Swanwick, the noted suffragette, also played by myself –

Donna But Tina gets silly sometimes –

Mordechai Thurrock – remonstrating with Joseph to keep Walter's memory pure –

Donna – and her conversation tends to have a narrow range, y'get me?

Mordechai Thurrock 'You must never tell, Joseph, you must never, ever tell!'

Miruts Oh, I know all about a narrow range of conversation . . .

Mordechai Thurrock The show also examines Sickert's place in the pantheon of great British artists, unjustly neglected in my opinion, his influence on the British avant-garde, his attraction to London's demi-monde . . .

Carlton Heroin makes you a good lover. Iss a fact.

Mordechai Thurrock The play explores the extraordinary dichotomy of Victorian Society –

Carlton Makes you slow and numb and less likely to spurge too soon . . .

Mordechai Thurrock – futuristic inventions and new medicines jostling next to imperialist barbarism and unfettered sexual aggression visited on the underclass . . . It's a comedy.

Carlton Makes you feel your skin like velvet . . . My skin is like velvet, mate, have a stroke, go on . . .

Mordechai Thurrock hangs up.

Mordechai Thurrock Jesus help me . . .

Carlton I'm a better lover than a crackhead . . . Jesus, you don't wanna make love to a crackhead, they're so nervous . . .

Mordechai Thurrock (*to himself*) Something has surely got to give . . . Mordechai Thurrock, you're a tsunami of talent about to wash over this town and bring them to their knees . . .

Marcus comes back upstairs.

Carlton Hey, Marcus . . . You know you should be an actor.

Marcus Eh?

Casey Big strong handsome fucker. Action hero.

Mordechai Thurrock Do you have any change for the phone?

Carlton Save the planet from terrorists. Yipee-ki-yay . . .

Marcus No, I'm sorry. I do not.

Donna Why you here?

Miruts What?

Donna Why you here?

Miruts Don't understand the question, love.

Miruts sells some weed to a passer-by.
  Enter Jayson.

Jayson Y'alright there, Marcus? Where's Casey? In the club?

Marcus Yup. Wanna see her?

Jayson Nah. She disturbs my flow when I'm getting ready for a fight.

Marcus Please tell me you ain't took that fight on, Jayson.

Jayson You held your nerve, right, Marcus? Please tell me you held your nerve.

Marcus Course I held my nerve, iss only ice water I have running through these veins.

Jayson Forgive me if I seem sceptical.

Marcus So you took that fight on?

Jayson Course I took it on, manz looking to boy me, how can I not answer the call?

Marcus Jayson . . . Thass Mad Gypsy John you're fightin. Thass juss . . . thass juss rashness . . . He outweighs you by at least five stone . . . The man is a monolith . . .

Jayson Watch him when he's felled. You gonna hear that body falling for a day and a half. Gonna drop the hammer on that lunatic old fuck, truss me.

Marcus Please, Jayson. I got so much respect for your fighting skills, your courage . . . Mad Gypsy John don't feel pain.

Jayson He won't have to feel pain. I'm gonna separate his mind from his body. Gonna splatter that oblongata. Put him to rest.

Marcus Be careful, Jayson.

Jayson I gone way back in time for what I'm got prepared for the fella.

Benny comes on, followed by Seamus.

They begin their overlapping dialogue as indicated on below.

Goin back to Tom Sayers, / heavyweight champion of the world, 1860, man was only five feet eight inches and weighed about one hundred and eighty pounds but he knocked out geezaz left and right, his punches sounded like cannonballs being fired into brick walls, especially good at slipping the jab gettin in close and brockin up the floating ribs . . . He come down from the slums of Brighton to come to London to work on the new railway in St Pancras. First ever international heavyweight contest was him and a Yankee in Hampshire in 1860, and they tumped at each other thirty-seven bloodsoaked rounds till the Yankee's muckers all leapt in an pulled their man out – Tom was outweighed by three stones and still he put the damage on the Yank. When he retired, all the aristocrats put three grand together, thass a mythical amount a' money back in the day, and he bought up a pub, right there up across the street a little way down, and then Tom married a young slapper who already had kids and who juss carried on horning the fella till he drank hisself to the grave at the age of thirty-nine.

Marcus and Jayson pause until Benny's 'could only guess at' on page 53.

Seamus (*overlapping from 'Tom Sayers'*) Why do you hurt me like this, Benny? Haven't I been good to you? Haven't I been kind to you? Haven't we had fun this last year?

Benny Seamus . . . You juss choking me . . .

Seamus I don't! How do I choke you?

Benny I juss can't be myself around you, you always tryna change me or teach me and I don't always feel like being at school, Seamus, yeah? Sometimes I wanna spend my Sunday afternoon flopping around in pyjamas catchin up on my soaps, not dragged around to look at some ancient Swedish movie 'bout some clapped out professor on a road trip with his niece or some fuckin boring surrealist bullshit painting –

Seamus That was a phenomenal exhibition and you said you loved the one with the drooping clocks – *The Persistence of Memory.*

Benny I remember what the blasted painting's called! And lemme juss educate you, Seamus, let me juss teach you one thing, Beyonce got talent and depth too! She's not Shostakovich and she's not Schnittke but the girl can rock a tough hard jam and she can finesse a soul smooth love ballad and sometimes thass whass needed, Seamus, yeah? Doesn't always have to be dissonance and flatted fifths.

Seamus You know I can't hack all that camp nonsense, Benny, I hate camp, and –

Benny Beyonce is not camp! Beyonce is fabulous! She writes great tunes and she got a voice that could cut a diamond in half, and that stuff gets people dancing and laughing and connecting, and juss once in a while I wanna be able to hear it in the house that we s'posed to be sharing!

Seamus How long you been feeling this, Benny? Why didn't you tell me any of this before?

Benny Because you too busy readin out loud from Christopher fuckin Isherwood to fuckin hear me!

Seamus looks bewildered.

I ain't some social experiment. I ain't here to be improved upon. I ain't here to be tamed. I'm your lover. I'm the

fifty-fifty man, remember? And if you wanna keep me . . .
y'best start seeing what I can bring to this thing . . .
Cause I tell you what, Seamus, you juss scratching the
surface, mate . . . I got the wisdom of King Solomon and
knowledge of things that you could only guess at.

Pause.

Marcus And you reckon cause you read up on this guy
you gonna stand a chance against Mad Gypsy John.

Seamus So what about that boy you was with?

Jayson Sayers was always overmatched –

Benny Oh please . . .

Jayson – and he did it by focusing on the torso shots,
mate.

Benny So one-dimensional it's not even funny.

Jayson I'm gonna put him to sleep.

Benny So immature.

Jayson Body shots like a tranquilliser dart, y'get me?

Benny He was juss there juss to get you to take me
seriously . . .

Jayson Step outta trouble and then juss sneak 'em in . . .

Benny You got nothing to worry about.

Jayson Take away his reach and drop the uppercut
hammer bambam –

Benny He's a boy and I'm looking for a full man.

Jayson I got a right hand that'll bring out the bitch in
any man.

Benny But I ain't looking for a dad.

Jayson Don't watch my size, I'm walkin out with retirement money causa my scholastic endeavours.

Seamus Benny, I –

Marcus Well, boy –

Seamus You're the only thing that I've got . . .

Marcus Forgive me if I'm seemin sceptical . . .

Seamus You're so precious to me.

Benny So put down the cap and gown and less you and me get to being in love.

Seamus So . . . which one is Beyonce anyway?

Benny Oh Seamus . . . Less get home quick. I have so much to show you.

Val Hello, Jayson.

Jayson Uh . . .

Donna I see you on this corner. I see how you weigh and measure people.

Val It's Val.

Donna How you use language –

Val Elliot's mother.

Donna Why you here?

Jayson Elliot . . .

Miruts Here on this planet?

Val Elliot, your brother.

Miruts Why am I here, like why do I exist, what?

Jayson I don't know who you mean.

Donna Why you here on this block being a detriment to your own upliftment?

Miruts Whass it gotta do with you?

Val Did you get the letter I sent you?

Donna Whass it gotta do wimme?

Val If I hurt you, then . . .

Donna Mankind is my brother, thass what iss gotta do wimme.

Val I was very young, y'know . . .

Miruts Do me a favour . . .

Val Pure godless chatter filling up my head.

Donna Do y'self a favour.

Jayson This is quite common, your mind has crossed fantasy with reality and iss all got a bit confused and you think that I'm someone I'm not.

Miruts I bet you look good when you take off that hard hat.

Val I need to ask you to do something important for me.

Donna I look sensational when I take off my hard hat.

Jayson I have a fight coming up in the next hour, and I gotta save my strength, so –

Donna Why you out here?

Val Trust me, if had anyone else to ask, I would, believe.

Donna Tell me why you wanna go wasting all that natural potential and sensitivity?

Val Elliot's off the rails, Jayson. He's been running round with this, this . . . lunatic called Richard.

Miruts I can't believe you got the audacity to ask me that.

Val This kid comes from a whole underworld family.

Donna Audacity?

Val Big people. Leviathan crew.

Miruts Yeah, audacity.

Val Elliot idolises him like he's Indiana fuckin Jones or something, places him above all others . . .

Miruts What the fuck bizness is it of yours?

Val And things juss came to a head last week at his school . . .

Miruts What are you, Little Miss Save-the-Underclass?

Val Teacher caught him knockin out a draw of skunk weed round the back of the gym and he punched the teacher, they've expelled him from school, and he's with Richard every minute of the day. I know iss Richard whass got him dealing, but when I challenge him on it, he just looks at me like he's gonna stab me . . . I don't recognise him as being my son. I can see my son in you, Jayson. Same kind spirit. Help the boy.

Jayson I don't know the kid and sounds like I don't wanna know him.

Val Why you like this? Jayson, he needs a brother –

Jayson Don't we all, love.

Val You think you can block whass in your veins. You can't deny a blood link. Ain't for you to punish me, I can't be punished for ever for what I did.

Miruts And what you doin working on the underground if you so smart?

Jayson This is . . . I don't need this. I don't need this in my life at all.

Donna S'all I ever wanted to do, workin on the underground.

Jayson The only memory I have of you is my old man draggin me round to your house –

Donna I'm being of use, thass what I'm doing.

Jayson – and seeing the kid crawling round eating his own shit and being told he was my brother and to go and play with him.

Miruts Subterranean woman.

Jayson Go and play with him . . .

Miruts Troglodyte.

Jayson The kid was filthy –

Donna Helping the city to move.

Jayson – went to get a towel out the bathroom –

Donna Helping people get to where they s'posed to be.

Jayson – and you told me off, said I had to ask first.

Donna Iss a buzz.

Jayson You wouldn't even let me get a sugared yogurt out the fridge.

Donna The arteries of the city since 1860 onwards, now thass tradition, / my friend, thass service. Say what you like about them Victorian repressive religious closet whoremongers, but they got a lotta things done and the world is better for their innovations. /

Jayson (*overlapping from 'tradition'*) You were two years older than me, and juss cause my dad knocked you up, you thought you could treat me like dogshit stuck to your shoe. I don't know you, frankly I'm amazed you even thought I could help.

Miruts (*overlapping from 'innovations'*) Yeah, them Victorians were gangsters, no doubt.

Val Elliot has been passing bent fifties around to the local drug dealers –

Miruts Takes a cold hard resolve to enslave half the known planet.

Val – and then they threaten me on road, the only thing stopping them is the link with Richard, they're scared a' him and so am I.

Jayson You're talking too fast now and I think you should relax –

Val Things are electric for me and there's a buzzin in my ears won't go away . . .

Donna Thass why they couldn't dance or cook. Had to keep it all together.

Jayson Hey –

Miruts Only the Victorians could come up with a story like *Jekyll and Hyde* –

Val Like flies buzzin –

Miruts – cause thass how all them freaks was doing.

Jayson Whoa!

Val He's suddenly got a new motor car / he's driving round the area like he's a movie star with the sunglasses and the boombox and I beg the boy tells me not to worry about it that iss none a' my business but how can it not be my business I'm his mum and my hair's coming out in clumps and I've found a loaded gun in his sock drawer, I've found a huge brick of crack cocaine under his bed, and thousands and thousands a' pounds. I'm a Christian woman with crack in my house, and when I talked to him Satan must juss catch up in his head and he . . . he hit me . . . He hit me . . . my son. Spat on me. Called me a whore. I thought I'd punished myself enough, but no, it's gotta go on till I'm ashes –

Jayson It's gonna be –

Val – and the police the police the police will take him away and throw him into a dungeon and I can't cradle him no more never never . . .

Jayson OK . . . It's alright, Val. /

Val There was a day when your old man brought you round and we went to the park and you held Elliot in your arms and he stopped crying straight away, the minute he saw your face, and you went up to strangers and told them you had the best little brother in the world and you wouldn't let him go – you must remember that, Jayson.

Miruts (*overlapping from 'suddenly got a new motor car'*) When they got to Tasmania, manz used to cut the heads off the men and making the women wear them round their necks like a pendant. Same year you talkin 'bout the Metropolitan Line starting up, 1869, the last Tasmanian was dragged out from his grave and made into a tobacco pouch. Ain't no limits to the sickness of the European mind . . .

Donna and Miruts pause.

Donna (*overlapping from 'It's alright, Val'*) Incredibly sturdy design. Much people woulda been bombed if they hadn't huddled together in the Blitz.

Miruts Oh, no, don't bring up that bullshit Blitz –

Donna And I couldn't work with a better bunch a blokes than those blokes. We all get it done. We huddle together when we're down there, even though none of us will admit it, we can all feel a . . . supernatural presence, y'know? Long dead but still vex.

Jayson Get her away from here, this corner's upsetting her.

Jayson takes Val over to Erkenwald.

Miruts This whole city swimming in the ghosts of madmen who feel they shoulda got a better deal.

Erkenwald leads her away.

Erkenwald Come on, lady . . . I know this place could drive a sane man mad.

Song
    The asphalt can be unforgivin if you let it
    If you ain't givin you ain't gonna get it
    But sometimes the night sweeps down with a
       light-fingered caress
    And we drop our defence and we stop the fight
       and fuss
    Juss look to each other and see past the snarl
    Help each other juss for a li'l while
    Cause we was not born to tear and hurt
    Something sweeter and kinder in our heart
    Reach to me
    And I'll accept you
    Reach to me
    And we'll turn this asphalt into a field

Donna I dunno if iss the suicides from down the ages or the people they used hang on this very spot when Tyburn

got too backlogged – 1600s – drag 'em up here on an
open cart followed by all manner of rowdy geezers, all
singing songs, tryna keep the fella spirits up –

Miruts Last thing you'd need is some sorta cockney
singalong as you transporting to the gallows.

Donna My personal theory is that iss Mother Damnable.

Miruts Mother Damnable . . . Sounds like a rapper.

Donna She lived right on this spot, in a cottage, juss her
and her sullen old face, mixin up potions and telling
fortunes . . . They say the devil walked right up to her
house and let hisself in. And never seen to leave. Mother
Damnable was found dead as a doornail the very next
day – a fire still burning and a pot of herb and liquid
still bubblin . . .

Miruts I dunno 'bout you, but if I see Mother Damnable
down there when I'm waiting for a northbound I ain't
even stoppin for breath, I'll juss run down the tunnels
and bite my way through any man thass impedin my
progress.

Donna This whole part of the city is notorious for
witches . . . Mother Black Cap . . . Mother Red Cap . . .

Miruts Tryna scare me?

Donna Can't you feel their presence?

Miruts Lemme get this straight. You believe in ghosts . . .
but you don't believe there's a god?

Donna I believe in you for some reason.

Miruts Why?

Donna I have no fuckin idea. You got nice eyelashes,
I dunno.

Miruts So, uh . . . Do I get to see you without the hard hat?

Donna If you gimme one good reason why you out here. Messing up all that potential . . .

Miruts This is my potential. What else I'm gonna do? I'm from a genuine war zone, babylove. My street where I kick a football up against a wall been battered by tank fire and strafed up by fighter planes. Chaos claimin my homeland quicktime, believe. We had to pack up everything overnight . . . And once we arrive in this land, myself and my family receive a most ungentle welcome from Cockburn and his kind. A most violent and hostile reception. My old man he's Amhara man, a proud man, he's a professor of philosophy in Addis Ababa, but in this country he gotta be a minicab driver getting puked on, and then school is like sorta zoo for deranged orang-utans, ain't much learnin goin on here, and now we have this new racist liar Boris Johnson for a mayor, a man who feels he's entitled to refer to black people as flesh-hacking piccaninnies and cannibals –

Donna Bet you never voted, though –

Miruts Don't think I'll be engagin too closely in politics if that scumbag's around, so iss a natural thing that I gravitate to the shadow world.

Donna So you out here sellin harmful products that fill people with paranoia and robs them of their ambition.

Miruts So what about alcohol – if that ain't a Class-A drug, I dunno what is . . . Fags and booze still killin more people than all the illicit substances put together.

Donna Alcohol and cigarette ain't gonna put your backside in jail, this junk you selling is illegal.

Miruts Drugs already legal if you white and live up in Hampstead cause no copper ever pulling you over to sweep your pockets. I would have some respect for this argument if manz wanted to ban all drugs, thass wrong-headed but at least iss consistently wrong-headed, but juss sayin this set a substance is beyond the pale but this set a' substance we allow . . . Cocaine and ganja go to prison but fags and booze you alright wimme, well, this has no intellectual or moral foundation whatsoever, darlin.

Donna I fail to see exackly what kinda intellectual and moral foundation you plantin by acting like a scrunty li'l knucklehead who ain't got the good sense not to tangle hisself up in madness out here.

Miruts Boy, I feel like my point can't penetrate unless I drop it in a syncopated lyrical perspicacity . . . Have a shufti at this, beautiful, see if I can't mek yuh change yuh stance.

> (*Raps.*) The war on drugs is just a war on blacks
> Criminal politicians juss don't know how to act
> The war on drugs is juss a war on blacks
> Criminal politicians juss don't know how to act
> Long-term unemployed
> Your confidence destroyed
> And the needle and the crack getting harder to avoid
> Cause the drugs is getting cheaper
> Prisons packing up with people
> Can't even get a job as a fuckin street-sweeper
> Brutalised set-aside prison living crucifies
>
> The war on drugs is juss a war on blacks
> Criminal politicians juss don't know how to act
> The war on drugs is juss a war on blacks
> Criminal politicians juss don't know how to act
> Whole thing is a fiasco

Iss all to do with cashflow
Prison population grow
We're going up in crack smoke
Ain't it strange
No needle exchange
And the brothers on the street are just dyin in vain
Junkies need treatment
And you buildin prison cells
Drug legislation makin life a livin hell
Oh my days,
Iss the CIA
Dropping off their package walkin quietly away

The war on drugs is juss a war on blacks
Criminal politicians juss don't know how to act
The war on drugs is juss a war on blacks
So open up your mind and read up on the facts
This war is juss a farce and iss totally unwinnable
A sea thass unswimmable
A ship thass unsinkable
So don't you think iss time that we think the
    unthinkable?
We wanna live like equals
Stop targeting my people
Make all the drugs legal
So we can all feel hope again
A message of love from the handsome Ethiopian

The war on drugs is juss a war on blacks
Iss juss a big fat lie
Like the war in Iraq
The war on drugs is juss a war on blacks
I'm an educated thug
With a rebel syntax

Donna Boy, you are exhausting and exasperatin . . .

Miruts Then whatchou still talking to me for?

Donna It's the eyelashes . . . They promise much . . . Less go somewhere.

Miruts Go somewhere and do what?

Donna takes off her hard hat.

Come round the corner. I got a place we can talk bout gentler things.

They exit.

Erkenwald Oh, we got some libidinous endeavours in the air . . . Can you feel it? Miruts about to make love for the last time before his death . . . Tell you what, people, less take a break, you can have a tinkle and getch'self a lovely homemade lemonade and we'll come back and tell you the rest of the story, how's that for a plan?

The band play something funky and uplifting.

End of Act One.

Act Two

Song
>We live in neon
>We live in concrete
>We're on the frontline
>With a broken heartbeat
>
>Lord knows the city
>Can take a heavy toll
>Vultures flapping overhead
>Gotta hang on to your soul
>Sometimes when the predators
>Show us their teeth
>No time to hesitate
>No time to feel grief
>
>We live in neon
>We live in concrete
>Our hearts get pounced on
>But we never admit defeat

Erkenwald He's taking her to a place not so far . . . Past neon and urine and hypodermics . . . Into his flat . . . Small but clean and restfully lit . . . And she's into it, cause she thinks she can heal him and change him . . . They give each other to each other . . . They collide . . . And when iss done, thass where they go . . . A tiny balcony with a dazzlin vista . . . See them there? Beautiful.

Miruts That church place is on fire still.

Donna Whole series of fires. Look.

Miruts Pass me a light for this.

She gets him a light for a smoke.

Donna You're in trouble aren't you? You done something wrong. Something with that older guy that was there earlier. You don't think you can make it right. You don't even wanna make it right. You can't see a way out.

Miruts The Queen of Ethiopia, Makeda, made a, made a pilgrimage to Jerusalem to see King Solomon cause he s'posed to know stuff, and when she gets there, Solomon gets one look at her and suddenly he ain't all that wise. She's beautiful, she's got to be his. He gets his cooks to load her food up with pepper and salt and to remove any drinking water from her quarters. Makeda knows whass going on, she ain't no fool, she's the queen, she reckons she can outlast the fella and go without water, but that pepper and that salt juss dryin up her throat till she runs into Solomon's quarters and asks for juss a solitary drop of water. And Solomon tells her she can have water just as soon as he has her body, and thass how they get a son, Menelik.

Donna Can I talk to the guy? Nobody's all bad, Miruts. If I talk to him, maybe he won't have to take such a hard line on you. What did you do? How stupid was it?

Miruts But you know that Menelik, growing up in Ethiopia, he wants more and he won't let it go. He goes to Jerusalem at the age of twenty-five and he takes what he thinks is his – he takes the Ark of the Covenant.

Donna Don't you understand?

Miruts Brings it back to Axum, thass where it is. Indiana Jones was a eedyat, iss still over in Ethiopia.

Donna I don't even know why, but I think I can be the thing that turns you around. Gimme a chance before it all gets too hot. Juss go to him and give it all back to him . . . Give him his gear and less bygones be bygones. No deed is so bad that it can't be forgiven. And no man is so low that he can't forgive.

Miruts Iss mine now. Iss mine.

Donna Miruts . . . I gotta go . . . Start work, sort out the fire damage on the lines . . . Miruts . . . I won't forget you, Miruts . . .

> *Donna leaves.*
> *Miruts tears up the package and hurls it off the balcony, sending a shower of cocaine into the night.*

Song
  We swagger and strut
  On broken bones
  We steal and rob
  The invisible ones
  We getting high
  Till our eyes pop out
  And you wonder why
  We always scream and shout
  Invisible
  Invisible
  We're desperate and we're invisible
  Invisible
  Invisible
  Y'all still don't hear me though

Mordechai Thurrock Hi, Cressida, it's Mordechai Thurrock again . . . I just want to say that we've only got the one week to run, and tickets really are selling like water, in fact it's like the Holy Grail, London is just ablaze talking about my show and I really, really think you *need* to see the show, not just because I'm keen to strike up a communication with you, but actually just because . . . Well, my acting and my work, yeah, will actually touch you in a deeper place than you've been touched before and you *need* to see it for your own emotional development, and that's the urgent truth, Cressida, you need to see it or you'll actually have no idea how to proceed with the rest of your life . . .

Carlton
I
Fuckin
Admire
All
You actin sort
Thass clever thass creative
I done a bit
School
I were good
But
Howjuh learn all those lines, like?
Howjou get it all in your brain?

Seamus scurries across the street, and indicates to Salim that he wants to do a deal.
Seamus is not very good at being cool and subtle.
Salim and Seamus disappear to transact. They are watched by Polish Jodie, who follows them with alacrity.

Violet Call y'self a man?

Marcus What? What did I do?

Violet Fuck all. You did fuck all.

Marcus What?

Violet Couldn't even intervene. You let me get gripsed up by some lunatic white supremacist and you froze up like an Amstrad computer.

Marcus I was getting ready to buss some moves on that fella, don't study me, girl, I'm a lion when I'm roused, I fight like a wounded panther when I'm ready, truss meh –

Violet Bottlejob.

Marcus Uh . . . Erkenwald and Mahmoud had it covered.

Violet Stop it. Juss own it. Say you're sorry.

Marcus I'm sorry. You know I wouldn't let anythin happen to you.

Violet Hum.

Marcus Friends?

Violet Come to think of it, I don't think I've seen you get stuck in once the whole time you've worked here. Left most of the takedown work for Bigboss to do.

Marcus Rubbish.

Violet No, iss coming clearer, I ain't never seen you putting your hands on anybody in here. What exactly are your qualifications for this job, if you don't mind my asking?

Marcus buries his head in his book.

Marcus? Put down your book and answer the question.

Marcus I don't choose to discuss this with you at this moment in time.

Violet Marcus, have you ever been in a fight?

Pause.

Oh, this too much. Adorable. You are so adorable. I thought you were cute before this, but now I just wanna wrap you up and spoil you.

Marcus Shut up.

Violet What are you gonna do, hit me? I been in more fights than you have.

Marcus I've been in sparring contests.

Violet Sparring contests? Was it pro? Where were these sparring contests?

Marcus In the dojo of my martial arts club. Where I learn discipline and valour.

Violet I've seen where you train, thass juss a lotta pattercake, ain't no sparring going on, you don't touch each other.

Marcus This conversation is beneath me.

Violet You are so cute. I can't believe it. A bouncer who don't know how to fight. Liddle soft poodgy-woodgy Marcus.

Marcus goes back to his book. Violet rips it out his hands.

Marcus Violet . . . gimme my book back.

Violet Fight me for it.

Marcus fumes impotently.

Marcus Gimme my book back, please.

Violet Arx me out and I'll give your book back.

Marcus I don't wanna ask you out.

Violet Bollocks. I seen you looking at me. My radar's picked you up nuff times. You want me.

Marcus I juss want my book back.

Violet Open up your mind, Marcus. Get brave. Get nasty.

Marcus See, you using language like that . . . Thass juss puttin out more pollution into the air. All that is . . . is static. Can't receive the Bigger Thoughts cause a' that rude stuff. Please gimme my book back.

Violet Whass the fear? You not been with many women?

Marcus This line a' questioning is really now a violation of my privacy, and I'd like you to desist if you don't mind.

Violet Scared of us? You should be. We burn down whole cities when we're ready.

Marcus The book, please.

Violet I'd break you in so gently. Teach you ev'rything.

Marcus You go from crudeness to crudeness and it's really very enervating.

Violet Ah, take your book, you virgin.

She gives him the book.

Marcus I'm not a virgin.

Violet Not int'rested any more. You're too much like my dad. Misery.

Marcus starts to read again. Pause.

Marcus Whadjuh mean, you're not int'rested any more?

Violet Juss read your book, Marcus.

Pause.

Marcus I'm sorry if I –

Violet Read the stupid book and leave me alone!

Marcus I feel bad now.

Violet If you don't read your book and be quiet I'm gonna read it to you!

Marcus Aloud?

Violet Shut up.

Marcus I might like that.

Violet Pervert.

Marcus You're fuckin nuts, you are.

Violet Don't swear.

Marcus See? Thass how much you exacerbate me. Make me use foulmouths. Ain't sworn since I was a kid.

Violet disappears into the club.
    Marcus settles back into his book.
    Donna enters in her hard hat and work bib, followed by Ragdale.

Ragdale You were far and away the bravest, brightest most enchanting child the world has ever known and I am delivered from purgatory by our reunion, daughter.

They disappear off, Donna moving fast to put distance between them, Ragdale struggling to keep up.
    Benny runs on.

Benny Scuse me . . . Have you seen a good-looking Irish fella round here?

Marcus shakes his head, 'No.'

He juss popped his first pill and I think he's spinning out.

Marcus shrugs: 'Can't help you, sorry.'
    Benny takes off.
    Roderique creeps up behind Beth.

Roderique A ghost.

Beth spins round.

Beth Oh, Jesus.

Roderique No. Roderique. Close, but not quite.

Beth Stay away.

Roderique I'm all the way over here, what threat do I pose, sugarplum?

Beth Don't you make a move in my direction or I'll scream for a copper.

Roderique So I'm down under the bridge looking at the water and I hear this voice carrying out . . . that dangerous voice make you wanna die . . . singing praise . . . You are a siren for true . . . Had no choice but to seek you out, girl . . .

Beth Leave me.

Roderique Come now . . . less put all the fire and brimstone stuff to bed for a little while, shall we? Iss good to see you. And I'm glad you cleaned up and all that. Truly. You know I always cared for you, Beth . . . You was a special part of my past . . . A positive motivating force within my life . . .

Beth You just tryin it on cause you looking to claim me.

Roderique Nah, love, on the real . . . Losing you was like losing a limb . . . Things ain't been all that conducive since you was last runnin this manor with me . . . things get darker, things get harder . . . These young chickens out here, they . . . they juss lack the depth you had, you know? They lack your brio . . .

Beth Heard you stabbed up a man over by the canal.

74

Roderique Oh Beth . . . I stabbed up many a man over by the canal . . .

Beth Thass the devil's claw you sittin in, Roderique . . .

Roderique I toldjuh iss harder out here now . . . Used to have structure but the youth make it chaotic. They think iss all a frickin PlayStation ting out here . . . think it ain't gonna hurt . . . Everything been amped up past the dial till iss distorted . . . Maybe you can gimme some a' that celestial vibration you been bangin on about . . . Is there space for a hopeless sinner?

Beth Jesus loves you. So I don't have to.

Roderique Come on Beth . . .

Beth Juss . . . let me be, Roderique.

Roderique Come on . . . Why you freezin me out? We got summink thass worth reviving, ain't we?

Beth Don't . . .

Roderique Come on . . . 'member that time I had that toe got all infected and you called it the toe of death? And 'member when I took the bandage off and made you smell the pus and you had to run to the bath and pour hot water down your nose till the stench left you? Thass . . . Thass teamwork . . . Thass intimacy . . . We fuckin laughed all night . . . Don't tell me there's any point in your life that you ain't gonna laugh about that . . .

Beth Thass juss . . . thass juss a memory . . . That ain't summink thass gonna resurrect a love . . . what, we had a few giggles? Course we had a few giggles, we wuz together for two years . . . But so what?

Roderique Iss not juss a memory, iss a foundation, iss a . . . iss a place that we built together, iss a culture thass juss yours and mine and no one else's and I ain't ready to juss put it to bed, lover, I still wanna wake up next to your morning breath –

Beth Stop. We was junkie thieves together and there ain't much thass less dignified and magical than a coupla addicts running around causing all kindsa various nefarious and murky misdeeds . . . wickedness unto others . . . You and me robbed little old ladies coming out the post office, we broke into people's houses and we stole their belongings, we terrorised people, we went days without speaking the truth . . . How you think summink like that is gonna work?

Roderique This connection is the only part of my whole life worth hanging onto. You used to make me laugh like it was going outta fashion and I miss you like I don't know what . . . I juss wanna be friends widjou . . .

Beth Shut up.

Roderique Save me . . . Make me whole again . . . I wanna be an innocent . . . I wanna be a good man . . . Bess . . . My lovely Bess . . . You can make me fly above all this crap if you juss lemme touch you . . . You're so special to me, Bess . . .

Beth Why you even still around these sides? This is the abyss. Why ainchou moved on?

Roderique So this fella, this Kurt fella, whass the flex with this fella, B?

Beth Whatdjou mean?

Roderique Like is he gonna breed you a coupla warriors for Christ and keep you fat in your dotage? Is he the one that's The One?

Beth Kurt is a blessing to my heart and I really don't feel all that easy bringing the man's name into this conversation we're having, Roderique.

Roderique Y'know you gonna be the mummy to end all mummies, Beth . . . I always reckoned it would be my li'l sprog you'd be bouncing on your knee.

Beth You getting a little free and easy widjour physical proximity and I'm asking you to give my persona some distance . . .

Roderique Oh man, there it is . . . there's that smell like orchid and sea salt . . .

Beth Roderique . . .

Roderique You the habit I can't break . . .

Beth Roderique.

> *Roderique produces a syringe full of heroin.*
> *He approaches . . .*
> *She extends her arm.*
> *He injects her.*
> *They kiss . . .*

Song
    Angels and fiends
    Both tearin at me
    I love
    I rise
    I die
    Earth
    Fire
    Lost
    God
    Love
    Dark
    Bleed
    Light
    Broken
    Broken

Love
God
Lost
Angels and fiends
Both tearing at me
Tearin at me
Tearing at me
Angels and fiends

They melt away.
   Babydoll, sixteen, enters and heads for the door of the fantasy bar.

Marcus Ohhh . . . Good evening, love, I think you must be in the wrong place.

Babydoll This where women take off their clothes?

Marcus Uh . . . yeah . . .

Babydoll Then I'm in the right place.

Marcus I don't think so, love, this is a place for adults only.

Babydoll When's he gonna get here?

Marcus I don't know, but he never hires under-age girls.

Babydoll I'm legal and I can do what I want.

Marcus If you say so, love, but . . .

Babydoll But what?

Marcus You must have a dad somewhere.

Babydoll So?

Marcus Well . . . If you were my li'l girl, I wouldn't want you anywhere near this place.

Babydoll Whass your name again?

Marcus I'm the bouncer, I don't need a name as far as you're concerned.

Babydoll You're a very handsome man, Mister Bouncer Man.

Marcus I think you should go home.

Babydoll I'm not a kid!

Marcus Alright.

Babydoll I'm a woman.

Marcus Fair enough.

Babydoll I'm all woman.

Marcus Good.

Babydoll I know you have a name.

Pause.

When's he coming? Feels like forever.

Marcus Is he expecting you?

Babydoll Yes. He's definitely expecting me. Alright, he's not expecting me.

Marcus I think you should go home.

Babydoll I wanna work here.

Marcus Go home, kiddo.

Babydoll I wanna be a dancer in this gaff.

Marcus I gotta say . . . it would be a mistake.

Babydoll Bet I'm prettier than any of the women you got in here.

Marcus Go home.

Babydoll Any of the girls you fancy?

Marcus Go home before he comes.

Babydoll One week in here and I bet I'm practically a millionaire!

Marcus There's a very sad ghost in this place.

Babydoll I'm well much too old to get scared by silly stories.

Marcus The man you're waiting for, the man you want to show your body to . . . He did something horrendous to this girl. And now she wanders around upstairs and sometimes you can hear her sing only she don't form no words too good on accounta she ain't got no tongue.

Babydoll No tongue?

Marcus No tongue.

Babydoll What happened to her tongue?

Marcus Bigboss did something horrendous, I told you.

Pause.

Babydoll You're chattin baer fuckries.

Marcus Ask any of the girls when they get here.

Babydoll Stupid ghost story . . .

Marcus tries to settle in to his book. He squints and winces in pain.

Whassamatter with your face?

Marcus Lotta headaches.

Babydoll Someone knock you out or summink?

Marcus No . . . No, I get them on accounta my reading all the time.

Babydoll So don't read. Matter fixed.

Marcus I have to read otherwise I won't get to the next level.

Babydoll What next level? There ain't no next level.

Marcus If I ain't got the words, yeah . . . If I don't know the words . . . then how am I gonna think Bigger Thoughts?

Babydoll What bigger thoughts?

Marcus I dunno, I ain't had 'em yet . . . But they're coming, believe. And when they do . . . Oh boy . . . Watch out for 'em.

Babydoll Words and thoughts are different things, though.

Marcus How you gonna organise a thought if you don't have words, though? Huh? You ever cogitate on that?

Babydoll You think you can find a word for everything? What about that moment juss before a kiss with tongues? What about a tower block sunset? What about when you wake up and you're miserable and a small child come up to give you flower they picked juss for you, you telling me there's words for how that make a person feel?

Marcus Go home

Babydoll Are you sure you don't wanna mess around wimme? I'm very discreet.

Marcus I find the very notion quite abhorrent.

Babydoll I like how you talk.

Marcus Go home.

Babydoll Come on . . . You're fascinating . . . You're so chivalrous . . . let's you and me have a little bit of fun, eh? Craziness. Crazy crazy craziness.

Marcus Go home.

Ragdale enters. He sees Babydoll and gasps in shock.

No, no, no, no . . . Not tonight, alright, Captain? Gimme one night off from this.

Ragdale I can't believe I've found you.

Babydoll Believe it, Grandad, cause here I am!

Ragdale Oh my precious child . . . Oh my joy . . . My love . . . We have so much to do together.

Babydoll I dunno about that, Grandad, you sure you ain't got a cross line?

Ragdale I love you, child. I can forgive you anything if you can forgive me.

Babydoll Forgive you? I wouldn't be so presumptuous. You got to forgive yourself, darling.

Ragdale I was so distant from you . . . I didn't know what was important . . .

Babydoll Thass alright . . .

Marcus Buster . . . can't you see? All the other birds you keep saying are your daughters . . . are much older. This is a teenage girl.

Babydoll Teenage woman.

Ragdale You have your mother's eye.

Babydoll Mother's eye? Just one?

Ragdale The left one. Quite uncanny. She'll be ecstatic.

Violet enters.

Violet Don't want any trouble from you tonight, old ma—

Violet looks at Babydoll in shock.

Oh God . . .

Ragdale Finally. Do you remember me?

Violet What's she doing in here? You let her in, Marcus? What's she doing in here?

Babydoll Don't get so aerated, Vi.

Violet What do want from here? What the fuck you doing coming to my place of business? Stay the fuck up out my business, Babydoll! Toljuh before.

Babydoll I wanna see where it is you go when you're not wimme and I got the two li'l uns on my frikking lap waiting for you.

Marcus This is your daughter?

Ragdale I'm a grandfather! Behold! I'm a grandfather!

Violet Get rid of him, Marcus.

Ragdale It's a dream to find you again after so many years.

Marcus I can't until he does summink untoward.

Ragdale We will go home together. I will leave you in the corridor while I speak to your mother. I will tell her that we have company and she will tell me to send them away, she will say, 'Why, old man, you really are the most tiresome creature.' And, and then I'll let you come in. And then . . . then she will bloom like a flower in June . . . I know it. And she'll dance around the room, no arthritis will stop her dancing. She'll dance and dance with you, we'll dance for you both . . . a waltz . . . And you'll clap along with us as we show you the old ways of dancing.

Babydoll This sounds proper heavy, blood. Less go and do it, Vi.

Violet Shut up. Get home. Marcus, why did you been sitting with her? You can tell she's under-age.

Marcus Safer talkin wimme than standing out here, specially a pretty li'l thing like that.

Violet Bollox. You tryna fuck her, weren't ya?

Marcus Your tongue should drop outchour mouth for saying that to me. She's a kid.

Babydoll He did try it on wimme, Vi.

Marcus Whaaat?

Violet I knew it . . . I could smell the nonciness on you from when you first come in here. What kinda fucked-up man sniffs around li'l sixteen-year-old girls?

Violet whips out a blade.

Babydoll So, pops, you saying you my grandad, then?

Ragdale I am your lollypop grandad and you are about to be spoiled beyond your wildest imaginings.

Marcus I never touched your daughter, Violet. Look at me. You know I wouldn't do that.

Babydoll He grabbed my backside and tried to take me downstairs. (*To Ragdale.*) So what was Vi like as a li'l girl? Was she fractious?

Ragdale She had an indomitable spirit and she would try anything, without trepidation.

Babydoll Really? Why she telling me off all the time?

Marcus Come on, Violet, does what she's saying tally with what you know about me? You know how scared I am of women.

Violet She's a li'l girl.

Babydoll Excuse me, but I am an adult woman of mystical proportion! Tell her, Grandad. Tell her I'm a woman.

Ragdale We have to come together as a family. We just need to keep talking to each other with honesty.

Marcus I am not a nonce! The idea is abhorrent.

Violet I seen how you look at me.

Babydoll You gonna gimme a World War Two liquorice, Grandad?

Marcus At you, maybe, but not at some li'l kid.

Ragdale Ah, the war . . .

Violet So you do look at me! I knew it! You watch me when I do my dances!

Ragdale How we danced in the war . . .

Marcus Course I don't! I watch the punters, make sure they don't put their hands on you, I'm not getting a free pervy look, thass beneath me, that is.

Violet All men are worthless and weak.

Marcus That may be true to a certain extent, but the salient point here is that I did not, nor will I ever, try it on with your adolescent daughter.

Violet Babydoll, tell me the truth. Did Marcus put his hands on yuh?

Babydoll Course not. Any yati wit two eyes can see Marcus is decent peoples.

Violet So whyjuh tell me he did?

Babydoll What, I gotta have a reason to make up a lie now? I don't think so.

Ragdale I need you to come home. Your mother is poorly. She's taken to her bed. Calls for you all the time. I think she's slipping into some kind of dream world. You're all she wants. She talks about the loss, she talks about the guilt, she talks about the regret.

Violet You persist with your sick mad bollocks any further and I'll throw you out of here myself and I won't be gentle like the virgin Marcus would be – you clear on that, you scaly fucking lizard-skinned degenerate nutter? You are not my father. You are not well. You are not wanted.

Marcus Come on, love, I think you've proved your point. Ease up on the old fella, eh?

Ragdale You have no idea how much pain you cause me with your words.

Violet You in pain? Good. My desired effect is what you get.

Ragdale You can't deny me for ever. I'm your blood. You must obey your blood.

Marcus Come on, sir . . . Let's leave her to it. She's just in a truculent frame of mind today.

Ragdale I am leaving to return. I will return with documents and photographs that will prove our connection incontrovertibly.

Ragdale hurries off.
Violet looks at Babydoll.
Babydoll looks at Violet.

Violet So. You're a woman now.

Babydoll Thass right.

Violet Think you can come to your old mum's place a' business and embarrass her.

Babydoll I ain't here to 'barrass you, I'm here to get some work.

Violet Work? You're sixteen, whatchou know about work?

Babydoll Don't condensend me, I'm ready for this – it can't be that hard if you're doing it.

Violet What did I ever do to you that you hate me so? What? Please explain because I really wanna know.

Babydoll You think this is summink to do wiyou and it ain't. Iss got fuck all to do wiyou, Violet.

Violet Never Mum. Always you have to call me Violet.

Babydoll What the fuck difference does it make if I call you Chang Hi Shek? And somehow the debate veers back to you and not to me. You reckon this thing is a movie and you're the lead role. So I'm juss following suit, but I'm the star now, I'm gonna be a dancer in this gaff, I'm gonna make the money, I'm gonna live my life the way I want to, and there is absolutely nish you can do about it. How you can come in here, make money and then tell me not to do it? Huh?

Violet If this is about money, then take it, look, here's loads of it, have it, go on, if iss gonna get you out of here then have it all, girl, but don't stay here because this is a place where women get . . . women get very tired, and I don't think you want that. You're too young to get tired.

You're too young to have dreams about eyes on your ceiling.

You're too young to hate men like a virus. You think this is some sorta movie I'm starring in? Well, where's the fuckin director to yell out 'Cut'? Where the fuck is he?

I'm getting old in here, daughter, my heart is like iss ninety-fuckin-four, gonna cave in any minute now. Go home, Babydoll. Please.

Pause. Babydoll bends down and scoops up the money Violet threw.

Babydoll Don't be chucking your money about like iss gonna persuade me of anything.

Violet I'm sorry.

Babydoll I'm keeping this, by the way. But thass not what swayed me.

Violet Alright.

Pause.

Babydoll You're not a bad mum. Not by any stretch of the imagined.

Violet Thank you.

Babydoll Not a great mum, mind. Not yet. Lotta work still needs doing.

Violet Li'l uns with my mum?

Babydoll Yeah. She's most probly about to catch a cardiac.

Violet Best go and get 'em, then.

Babydoll OK, Mummy.

Pause.

Violet Getchourself summink nice widat money. Not tarty stuff. Buy summink nice.

Babydoll Alright.

Violet Alright.

Babydoll exits.
Marcus re-emerges.

What you looking at?

Marcus She's a nice girl. Juss like her mum.

Violet I know you didn't get funny with her, Marcus.
I juss wanted to pull a blade on you, thass all.

Marcus I'm flattered.

Violet Boy, you don't even know how your whole future
in the balance right about now . . . You could be fulfilling
your destiny wimme . . . Or you could spend the rest a'
your life going, 'I coulda had her! I coulda had her!' He
who hesitates is lost.

Marcus Well, lemme hesitate on that a li'l longer.

Violet exits.

Mordechai Thurrock Hi, it's Moredechai Thurrock here
trying again for Cressida, and for the last time, because to
tell you the truth, yeah, I'm feeling a little exasperated,
yeah, I'm feeling more than a little peeved, I've spent a
lot of time really . . . *digging* around in some fairly scary
unpleasant corners of my mind to research this show
about Walter Sickert the great Impressionist painter,
yeah, a lot of pain and a lot of sacrifice has gone into it,
yeah, if I'm being completely candid with you, which I
think we should be with each other, *I am fuckin pissed off
and insulted! You dare to brush me off at my showcase!
If you can't see what I have to offer this industry, if you
can't see what I'm offering to this city, to this world,*
then . . . Y'know there'll come a night when you'll open
your front door, plop your keys down and flop onto

your sofa fumbling for the TV remote and that's where
I'll be . . . And, boy, will it be a long time till the sun
comes up. Do you understand me? I'm going to hurt you
and hurt you and hurt you.

*Mordechai Thurrock's ten-pence pieces run out. He
flops down next to Carlton and bursts into tears.*

Carlton
 I went theatre once.
 To be honest, I didn't reckon it much cop.
 There were a lot of showing off,
 and when they talked to each other,
 they wouldn't look at each other,
 they'd look out front
 like as if
 they were talking to the audience
 and not each other,
 and I'd juss think . . .
 Juss,
 whassamatter with juss talking
 to each other, y'know?

*Mordechai Thurrock tucks himself under Carlton's
blanket.*

Thass it mate . . . Take your shoes off. You'd be more
comfy.

Carlton helps his shoes off.

See? Feels better, don't it?

Mordechai nods his head.

You curl up there, mate. Next to old Carlton. Carlton'll
keep you safe.

*Enter Polish Jodie, with Seamus, dancing. Seamus has
an unfeasibly fat spliff hanging out of his mouth and
is waving a conductor's baton. He can't stop laughing.*

Polish Jodie (*in Polish*)
Love has got me feeling so crazy right now
Your love's got me looking so crazy right now
Your touch got me feeling so crazy right now
Uh oh uh oh uh oh

Benny comes on, breathless, in pursuit . . .

Benny Come on, Seamus . . . Perhaps you swingin a little too hard to the pleasure dome . . .

Seamus (*in Polish*)
Got me hoping you page me right now
Got me hoping you'll save me right now

Polish Jodie gives Seamus a massive dirty snog.

Polish Jodie (*in Polish*) Hhhmmm . . . I'm going to make you see the face of God tonight.

Benny Hey, hey, get your tongue out of my boyfriend's mou—

Polish Jodie Ssshhhh . . .

She plants an enormous dirty snog on Benny – long deep and sexually intense.
   The kiss finishes.
   Seamus pisses himself laughing.
   Benny tries to speak but can't.
   Polish Jodie takes them by the hand.
   They exit singing.
   Jimmy comes running on. Looks to Marcus.
   Marcus points a finger in the direction that Polish Jodie, Benny and Seamus just went.
   Jimmy runs off.

Erkenwald Yuh look like yuh juss seen a woolly mammoth.

Marcus I been out here on this corner a while now . . . But every time I think I see it all . . .

Erkenwald I know, son . . . Iss juss fabulous.

Enter Ragdale, clutching his photo album.

Ragdale I want you all to look at these photographs in my hand.

Nobody notices.

Where are my daughters?

Marcus Old man . . . Lemme read my book tonight, alright? Thass all I wanna do.

Marcus goes back to reading his book.
  Ragdale fidgets.

Please don't fidget like that.

Ragdale You need glasses.

Marcus What?

Ragdale You're squinting at the page.

Pause.

Marcus Iss juss the print is small, thass all . . .

Ragdale Here.

Ragdale offers him his reading spectacles.
  Marcus reluctantly tries them on.

Marcus For pooh's sakes . . .

Ragdale Clearer, isn't it?

Marcus Yeah!

Ragdale Won't be such a struggle for you once you have some made up.

Marcus This is so much easier now!

Ragdale Excellent. Now you can tend to your studies instead of pretending you can fight.

Marcus You're not going to stop, are you?

Ragdale Of course I'm not going to stop. Would you stop if it was your child?

Marcus When did you last see her?

Ragdale Half an hour ago.

Marcus Captain . . . when was she last in the drum?

Ragdale Drum?

Marcus Drum 'n' bass. Place. Domicile. Home.

Ragdale She was fifteen.

Marcus How old is she now?

Pause.

Have you thought about . . . ?

Ragdale What?

Marcus The possibility . . .

Ragdale Possibility of what?

Marcus Possibility . . . that she's . . . that she's not alive.

Ragdale grabs him by the lapel.

Ragdale I would have known. I would have felt the exact moment. If her heart stops beating, then my heart stops beating. She is alive because I can feel her.

Marcus Me too, Captain. I feel her too.

Ragdale opens photo album and proffers it to Marcus.

Ragdale See? There are my children.

Marcus Captain . . . these pictures are old.

Ragdale They are the most precious possession. This is my child.

Casey comes up for a cigarette.

Daughter . . .

Casey Mister . . . If you keep on, I'm gonna make *you* my daughter.

Ragdale Impudent child.

Salim re-enters.

Erkenwald Hey. Young fella. Could we agree to keep it pacifistic tonight? My nerves are strained, son, eh? I know you're a nice boy underneath it all . . . And, uh, also . . . I heard down the flower stall that your mum's poorly again . . . Please send her my best, eh?

Salim Shut up. Manz get jooked for talking bout manz mum. Don't talk to me again. I'll flay your face to the skull.

Erkenwald Alright, son . . . have it how you want it.

Mahmoud Come here.

Salim goes over.

Have coffee. My treat. Have coffee.

Salim Whass all this?

Mahmoud Have coffee.

Salim Whassa catch then?

Mahmoud No catch. Juss drink coffee and talk wimme.

Enter Jayson. He is horrifically bruised and cut from a real going over.

Casey Jayson! What the fuck happened to your face?

Enter Kurt.

Salim I seen you on this block.

Jayson Put it this way . . .

Salim You don't give nobody nothing if they don't have correct cash.

Jayson It didn't go quite according to plan.

Salim Whadjuh want from me, blood?

Mahmoud Smart boy.

Kurt Where is she? My Beth.

Mahmoud Can see it in your eyes.

Kurt She's lost a lot of her paperwork.

Mahmoud But the Ehthiop is right.

Erkenwald You know where she is, kid.

Casey I toldjuh not to fight him.

Erkenwald Duuno why you're even askin me.

Mahmoud You don't know what you're supposed to be and your mind is squirming with confusion.

Kurt She with him?

Jayson He's a big gigantic handful, I give him that much.

Kurt She gone with him?

Salim Oh, juss what I'm needing . . .

Jayson But he cheated, Casey.

95

Erkenwald Yes, kid.

Salim I don't need a load of deep bollox right now.

Erkenwald She went with him.

Jayson Mad Gypsy John did not fight fair at all.

Erkenwald And you and me both know that she was always gonna go with him.

Casey Why would you think a man called Mad Gypsy John would fight fair?

Mahmoud Somalia, right? I been to Somalia.

Casey Summink in the name shoulda given you a clue, Jayson.

Salim Howjuh get from Afghanistan to Somalia?

Mahmoud taps the side of his nose – 'That's a secret.'

Mahmoud Northern Somalia.

Jayson I think he put some sorta pepper sauce on his knuckles or somesuch.

Erkenwald Inevitable, innit, son?

Jayson Cause I'm havin trouble seein out this eye –

Fuming under her breath, Casey wipes Jayson's eyes with a hankie.

Salim My folks are from the north before we moved to Mogadishu.

Erkenwald A blind man could see it a mile off.

Mahmoud Ahhh yes . . . so handsome you could only be a Dhulbahante. A dervish.

Erkenwald Robert Palmer was right, son. 'Gonna have to face it, you're addicted to love.'

Mahmoud What people you come from!?

Kurt Where does he live?

Mahmoud Ferocious.

Casey This is it.

Erkenwald Where does he live?

Mahmoud Relentless.

Casey No more boxing.

Erkenwald No particular place, son.

Mahmoud Disciplined.

Kurt grabs a beer bottle and smashes it.

Kurt Raaaahhhhh!!

Casey You retired.

Erkenwald Oh now thass juss silly, son . . .

Mahmoud Completely indomitable.

Kurt Gonna find him and, and, and, / and, and, and, and, and, and –

Mahmoud (*overlapping from 'and, and, and'*) Fought off the British and the Ethiopians for how long do you think?

Kurt Take him from this world.

Salim I don't fuckin know, man . . . You going on baer long.

Erkenwald Now whass that gonna solve?

Kurt Whass it gonna solve?

Casey I'm announcing your retirement.

Kurt Whass it gonna solve?

Mahmoud Twenty years! Twenty years.

Casey Press conference, everybody.

Kurt I'll drink his blood and end his life, thass what iss gonna solve! He took my Beth! Beeethhh!

Kurt exits purposefully.

Erkenwald (*sings*) 'Onward Christian Soldiers, marchin as to war . . .'

Casey Jayson's had enough of getting his brain sloshed / up against the side of his skull and wishes to call it a day and get some proper job. He's done with it. I mean it, Jayson. I don't care how much money you're making.

Mahmoud (*overlapping from 'sloshed'*) And as they fell, young men barely born when the resistance began would pick up their dead fathers' rifles and charge into battle.

Jayson Well, thass another thing . . .

Mahmoud Ethiopia couldn't handle the Dervish.

Casey Whass another thing?

Mahmoud The British couldn't handle the Dervish.

Jayson About payment . . .

Mahmoud And even when they forced them to flee, they never signed any traitor's treaty, not like the Warsangeli and the Issa.

Casey Jayson . . .

Salim Warsangeli Tribe can eat out my bum crack.

Casey Is this gonna upset me?

Mahmoud What do you think Sayyid Hasan would say if he could see a descendant of the Dervish out here doing what you do?

Jayson I looked for the guy, the whassit, the promoter, but he'd gone . . .

Casey Most probly gotta be back in a coffin before the sun comes up.

Carlton Doin my head in all this talk of violence.

Mahmoud You playing into the hands of the oppressor by fulfilling every prophecy they make for you.

Jayson I'll find him and I'll get my money.

Erkenwald I know what you mean, Carlton.

Mahmoud You turning y'self into a stereotype for the British.

Casey This ain't even about the money.

Mahmoud To look at and point at.

Carlton Upset me, make me take more gear.

Casey You keep doin this, and you're gonna end in one them chairs you gotta blow into a straw to move about the place, juss like poor old Clark Kent.

Erkenwald Yup. Best thing to do, son.

Casey I don't want you fightin, lover.

Mahmoud To point at and look at.

Casey Not even with guys your own weight.

Carlton But this is my last fix.

Casey It has to stop, lover.

Mahmoud One thing I will concede . . . One contribution these savages have made to world culture.

Jayson Babe . . . you're hackin off my bollocks one globe at a time.

Carlton All good things gotta come to an end.

Jayson What am I s'posed to live off?

Mahmoud The one thing they have done to make the world less tragic and barren . . . Marmite.

Jayson I ain't living off your money –

Mahmoud This really is the most extraordinary achievement . . .

Jayson Thass demeanin to my manhood, that is.

Mahmoud And one that remains shrouded in mystery . . . All you can find out . . . / Yeast extract, but most crucially a living yeast extract – which could not have been possible without Pasteur and a man named Liebig, a German –

Casey (*overlapping from 'all you can find out'*) So go into personal training, go into labouring, I don't give a fuck what you do –

Mahmoud Vegetable extract.

Casey – as long as it don't involve you catching big fists in your eyebrows, then I'm cool with it, but I'm telling you now, I ain't got no more room for violence.

Mahmoud Well, yes, but extract of which particular vegetables, do you know? I don't.

Casey You got nine months to get it together and then we're gonna be mummy and daddy to a new human being on this planet, Jayson.

Jayson Casey . . .

Mahmoud Niacin . . . Now, this is a nicotinic acid – nicotine!

Casey I mean it . . . My li'l baby ain't growing up with no toothless cauliflower-earholed punch-drunk shamblin donkey, y'understand me?

Mahmoud Spices, yes, but again which particular spices?

Jayson Casey . . . Whatdidyouwhatdidyouwhatdidyou say?

Mahmoud The yeast is from the offcuts of breweries, but is not alcoholic in composition –

Casey Start thinkin up names, lover.

Mahmoud – which is then given lots of salt to make it hypertonic or 'lysis' which shrivels up the cells –

Jayson Casey . . .

Mahmoud – which triggers a process called autolysis –

Jayson Casey . . .

Mahmoud – in which the yeast commit suicide and self-destruct, which is then heated to get the right texture.

Jayson You gonna be the best mother in the history of the world.

Mahmoud And what a taste!

Jayson Our kid's gonna be beautiful.

Mahmoud There is no self-pity at all in the flavour of a Marmite.

Casey If it's a girl she'll have my nose and your eyes and my lips, you don't really have lips to speak of, and your neck / and my ears and she'll be a stubborn li'l so-and-so, or course, coming out you and me but who would want it any other way?

Mahmoud (*overlapping from 'your neck'*) They bang on about, what's his name, Charles Darwin who by his own admission is nothing more than a circus freak, the Amazing Talking Ape from Shropshire –

Jayson I got lips. I got plenty of lips.

Mahmoud And these windbags Shakespeare and Dickens, bombastic narcissists with no ability to self-edit . . .

Casey And we can put a deposit down on a bigger place.

Mahmoud But when archaeologists sift through the rubble of the English society –

Casey I should be alright.

Mahmoud – what they will marvel at . . . will be Marmite.

Casey Pregnant women make much money in the clubs.

Mahmoud Democracy.

Casey We gonna need to move closer to some sorta decent school.

Mahmoud Democracy.

Jayson My old school ain't far from here, council might move us –

Casey and Jayson hug for the first time in the scene.

Mahmoud Any time you hear that word 'democracy' being used by politician person, it's not long after that some brown people going to be massacred.

Casey You're gonna need to get good at painting and decorating –

Mahmoud What a farce.

Casey – because this baby gotta have teddy bears all the way round the room –

Mahmoud Vote for the corporate puppet with the straightest teeth and the prettiest wife.

Casey – and we're gonna need to buy one a them things, whadjucallit –

Mahmoud Civilisation.

Jayson Mobiles.

Mahmoud Enlightenment.

Jayson They're called mobiles.

Mahmoud Progress.

Casey Thass it.

Mahmoud If they're left unchecked –

Casey Mobiles. One a' them.

Mahmoud – you will have to explain to your grand-children what an elephant was.

Casey I'm gonna need to re-take my driving test and pass this time.

Mahmoud What a tiger was.

Casey Jesus, I'm 'bout to explode with all this hope.

Mahmoud What a Palestinian was.

Jayson Our baby gonna be the most beautiful human being on the whole entire planet.

Casey How are them cuts on your nose?

Jayson They sting.

Casey Sting too much to be kissed?

Jayson Never could sting that much.

Casey I'm gonna kiss 'em then. Better?

Jayson Much better.

Salim Could we talk about this at a later date?

Casey What about that bruise upon your eyelid?

Salim I'm feeling kinda fragile and you're being very pushy about this whole thing. I heard your voice, yeah, and you struck a chord, yeah, summink in you chimed and so I wanted to give you a hearing –

Jayson It could really do with a kiss.

Salim – but you pronounce from on high about a lotta things and you talk about my life like you got all the answers and I don't like it.

Casey I love you like a flower loves rain. I gotta go and dance. You gonna be the kindest father.

Salim And y'know what, I kinda like it out here, it feels safe to me, this pageant, y'understand, old fella?

Enter Miruts. Salim sees him.

Mahmoud Don't go, young fighter. I want to tell you about the Unocal pipeline they build in my country . . .

Salim Hey, fassyhole.

Mahmoud As the plans for the pipeline start to build –

Salim I want words wiyou.

Mahmoud – the same pipeline that Unocal Delta wanted to build in the early nineties –

Miruts Oh Jeez . . .

Mahmoud – to get the oil from Kyrgistan –

Miruts You know you're like a turd that juss won't flush.

Mahmoud Turkmenistan –

Miruts Y'know that?

Mahmoud Uzbekistan –

Miruts Why don't you juss dive down into the sewer where you belong and leave us normal decent drug dealers alone –

Mahmoud – the last untapped oil resource on the planet –

Miruts You're messin up the whole vibe round here . . .

Mahmoud – potential five million barrels a day –

Salim Ordinary decent drug dealer?

Mahmoud – shipped out through our country –

Salim You the one juss stole a bunch of lemon barley off that lunatic ancient cockney braer.

Mahmoud – into the Caspian Sea –

Salim Thass a step toward the abyss, my friend, and you muss not wanna live.

Mahmoud – thus avoidin Iran and China.

Miruts Whether I wanna live or die or float somewhere in between, thass not your concern.

Mahmoud Great for them –

Miruts NOW MOVE FROM ME!

Mahmoud – but not so good for the ecology of our country –

Miruts I ain't in the mood for physical conflagration –

Mahmoud – and this strange inbred illiterate cowboy drunkard that sits drooling in the White House –

Miruts Y'understand me?

Mahmoud – when he was governor of Texas –

Miruts Juss move from me.

Mahmoud – made us his honoured guests –

Salim Ain't so brave when you ain't surrounded by your countrymen, are ya?

Mahmoud – before the deal collapsed –

Miruts You think I draw strength from a crowd?

Mahmoud – and Unocal unsatisfied –

Miruts I don't need no crowd a' people to bury you up to the neck for seagulls to pluck out your fuckin eyes, ya fassyhole pussyhole wanker.

Mahmoud – till now that our cities have been flattened once again –

Miruts Step to me if you think you're bad –

Mahmoud – and who wins the pathetic farce they call an election –

Miruts Juss step to me –

Mahmoud This errand boy Karzai –

Miruts Take one step further –

Mahmoud – and where did Karzai used to work? Unocal.

Salim Yeah?

Mahmoud This word 'democracy'.

Miruts Take one step further

Mahmoud Karzai can't leave his compound.

Salim Yeah?

Mahmoud If he's truly the people's choice –

Miruts Yeah?

Mahmoud – why does everyone want to kill him the minute he steps out of his front door?

The two young fellas get into a big fight. They are both extremely skilful streetfighters, trained in Eastern and African martial arts – capoeira, wing chun, hapkido – so, no matter how hard they try, they are actually unable to land a single blow on each other, even though they're flying around trying. Spinning kicks, jabs, feints, ducks . . . It's a big complicated fight.

Miruts You tired yet?

Salim Fuck no. You tired yet?

Miruts A little.

Salim Good. Cause I got a stitch.

Miruts Juss wanna stop moving juss for one minute.

They both stop.

Salim You really robbed that cockney fella?

Miruts What, is there some sorta ghetto Sky News about here broadcasting my day-to-day?

Salim That fella is truly a nuttah, y'know. Thass some old-time deep-rooted firm got plenty a' muscle to back it up. He kill you tonight, he'll be in South Korea runnin a sports clothes shop by Tuesday. New passport and everything.

Miruts Don't worry 'bout me.

Salim Miruts . . . I would truly hate to read that you got blooded and killed out here.

Miruts nods.

Miruts Are you some sorta poof or summink?

Salim Juss be careful, man. Get out the area for a little while at least. Gotta go. Gotta check on my mum. Them carers are watless . . .

Miruts Iss you that makes her poorly, you know that. Carryin on like you General Aideed . . .

Salim almost smiles.

Salim And iss you thass makin me poorly widjour belligerent wayz, Leggese Teffera . . .

Salim exits.

Mahmoud Qorma alou bokhara! Get your lovely Qorma alou-bokhara here!

Enter Cockburn. He bumps into Ragdale and Violet.

Ragdale Do you have no manners at all?

Cockburn looks at Ragdale.

Cockburn No, I don't.

Grabs the photo album out of his hand. Tears the photos to shreds.

There's your fantasies! There's your memories!

Ragdale is utterly distraught. He scrambles on his knees picking up the pieces of his treasured photo album.
Cockburn turns to Miruts.
Elliot runs on behind.

Well, well, well . . . A little thieving blind mouse nibblin for cheese up his own bum.

Elliot Miruts . . . Why didn't you run? /

Miruts I been hatin geezas like you since I got here . . .

Cockburn Thass juss fine cause I got more hate in my heart than you can comprehend, son.

Elliot Come on, old fella, let this one slide, eh? Bygones be bygones . . . He can juss give you the whole package back and thass all square, eh? I'll explain to Richard.

Cockburn Richard? You think I need Richard?

Erkenwald (*overlapping from 'Why didn't you run?'*) Some people juss never settle into the physical realm at all . . . They don't wanna have bodies, they don't wanna have consciousness, they'll do anything to have rid of it, they can't bear their own potential for beauty cause that would be something akin to freedom. See, Miruts ain't made an effort to run, he ain't made an effort to barter or do pretty much anything 'cept get high with the London Underground girl . . . And Cockburn . . . You don't fuck around with men like Cockburn.

Mahmoud That's right, you don't. Cockburn is terrible people.

Erkenwald There's no way he's gonna wear that sort of embarrassment . . .

Mahmoud Thass right, he won't.

Erkenwald And so now Miruts will be murdered.

Mahmoud Shame. Nice boy.

Cockburn pulls a gun and plunges it deep into Miruts's belly before pulling the trigger.
Miruts falls, not quite dead.

Everything stops.
Cockburn goes to leave.
Marcus blocks his path.

Marcus Hold on, mate . . . You ain't walking away from that . . . Thass a human life you juss took, not some piece of farmyard animal . . .

Cockburn Heheehh . . .

Marcus You may well laugh, mister, but your kinda people make me sick to breathe the same air with your hate and your violence and there ain't no place for you 'cept a dungeon and I'm gonna bring your racist self to justice.

Marcus drops into a martial arts crouch and emits a fearsome warrior cry.
Cockburn, amused, puts his gun in his pocket and beckons him forth.

Cockburn OK, big fella . . . Less be havin you . . .

Marcus makes to strike at him.
Cockburn ducks, headbutts, kicks Marcus in the balls, effortless, efficient, professional.
Marcus drops to the floor.
Cockburn stomps on him and stomps on him.
Violet moves forward with a small can of mace. She sprays him.
Cockburn staggers back and out. He exits.
Donna comes on and moves slowly and calmly to Miruts.

Miruts (*in Amharic*) Going home . . . Don't forget me, lover . . . going home . . . Put me to rest in my beloved Ethiopia.

He dies . . .
She holds him.

The Street completely stops.
A siren in the distance.

Song
　Tell Heaven
　Now you tell Heaven
　I am coming
　I'm coming on home
　Oh, one day
　Just tell my Heaven
　My Heavenly King
　Just tell him that I'm coming
　That I'm coming
　On the morning train
　Oh the river
　Lord know the river
　Where the sun
　That evening sun
　Never goes down
　Cross on my shoulder
　Sword in my hand
　I'm going down fighting
　In Jesus' name

Elliot Boy . . . I suddenly feel like I'm a thousand years old . . .

Jayson Iss Elliot, isn't it?

Elliot Uh?

Jayson You Val's li'l boy, right?

Elliot Yeah . . . Yeah, I'm Val's li'l boy.

Jayson I must reason with you. Take a stroll wimme.

Elliot He juss . . . he juss vacated his body . . .

Jayson Take a stroll, young Jedi.

They leave together.
Violet helps Ragdale gather up his photos.

Violet I think thass all of them . . .

Ragdale Look . . . There you are . . . see? Dressed in a sunflower costume . . . How happy you are . . .

Violet Oh yeah . . . there I am . . .

Ragdale Remember?

Violet Course I remember.

Ragdale And you wouldn't let me tie your shoelaces up, said my fingers too fat, said you wanted Mummy to do it.

Violet Fair's fair, she tied 'em up better then you.

Ragdale I beg your pardon, young lady, but she did not. When I tied them up, they never came undone again.

Violet Thass true.

Ragdale This was a happy time.

Violet Yeah.

Ragdale Before the madness.

Violet I remember.

Ragdale Like all fathers, I silently wished you'd never grow up . . . Just stay this age . . . I never wanted all the heartache to happen to you . . .

Marcus I think I got another scrap here for you.

Marcus, still recovering on the ground, hands Ragdale another scrap of photo.

Ragdale Now what are your intentions toward my daughter here?

Marcus Eh?

Violet Yeah, Marcus, what exackly are your intentions?

Ragdale Because I will not suffer to have her hurt, not by you, nor any other man. My wrath is terrible to behold.

Marcus Tell you what . . . I'll treat you to a hot dog, how's that? Erkenwald'll put it on your tab.

Erkenwald Will I fuck. I want money up front.

Marcus gives Erkenwald a look.
Erkenwald huffily relents.

Come here, Colonel, what can I fix yuh? The onions make the whole experience . . .

Ragdale shuffles over, clutching his photos.

Violet How's your ballbags, Marcus?

Marcus Uh . . . They're not too clever, Vi, no.

Violet Ice?

Marcus On my testicles? No thanks, love.

She helps him to his feet.

Violet Quite a kicking you took, kiddo.

Marcus All that training . . .

Violet You stood firm, Marcus. You took a stand and you stood firm.

Marcus Ain't standing too fuckin firm right now, tell yuh.

Violet All the time with the foul-mouth.

Marcus Do excuse me.

Violet helps him up.

Violet You mean the world to me tonight.

Marcus How old's your kids?

Violet Sixteen, six, and three.

Marcus My goodness.

Violet Wanna meet 'em?

Marcus S'pose I'd better.

Violet You a good dancer?

Marcus I shuffle about to no particular great effect. I'm telling you now, right . . . I've only had three girlfriends. One was at school, one came to karate for a while, and one was the teller at my local bank. They all dismissed me from service. All for the same reasons.

Violet Whassat?

Marcus Apparently I'm a profoundly boring man . . .

Violet You don't bore me. You intoxicate me.

Marcus Likewise, darling.

They go to kiss.

Erkenwald When a star in the sky dies, we keep gettin its light for another thousand years or so.
　　I sometimes wonder if thass what all this is.
　　All you're seeing.
　　Distant echoes from a long-dead star.
　　Black holes are just stars that burnt thesselves out and died but they don't know they've died and now they're looking to suck any living thing in.
　　Death gets lonely.
　　Death needs company.
　　Our city is on fire.

Can a city ever die?

Perhaps we should make way for the return of the woolly mammoth. They might do a better job of looking after their young than we're doing.

We thank you for stopping by.

Allowing y'self to be serenaded by the Desperate Invisibles . . .

Oh my goodness, what a lovely jig we have to send you home with.

The Band strikes up a jig.

Jig Song
    The frontline
    The frontline
    Never give up
    Never give up
    The frontline
    The frontline
    Never give up
    Never give up
    That's how we roll
    That's how we roll
    Empty pocket
    Beautiful soul
    The frontline
    The frontline.

    End.